1892

Race Course transformed with inauguration of new Clubhouse, Grandstand and Betting Ring, designed by Boston architect Herbert Langford Warren.

Horse Haven track lengthened to one mile circumference.

1903

Oklahoma – new training track and stables – built adjoining Horse Haven.

1911-13

Anti-gambling laws force closure of Saratoga and all New York tracks.

1901

Sanford Court, private stabling complex, built opposite Race Course property by carpet millionaires Stephen and John Sanford.

1891

Race Course changes hands again. Bought by Gottfried Walbaum, gambling-shop owner and President of Hudson County Jockey Club.

1908

Agnew-Hart Act passed, prohibiting the soliciting or recording of bets in a fixed place.

1917

Fasig-Tipton Co. begins annual yearling sales at Saratoga. Builds sales ring and paddock opposite Horse Haven.

1894

Nellie Bly, star New York reporter, launches exposé against Saratoga Race Course, branding the town "Our Wickedest Summer Resort". Reputation of track plummets.

1902

Race Course taken over by new management headed by William C. Whitney. Track is shifted and Grandstand is enlarged.

August Belmont Jr., financier and chairman of Jockey Club, builds Clare Court, a private stabling complex at Race Course.

1910

Amended anti-gambling bill restricts all forms of wagering.

TIMELINE

1919

Saratoga Association acquires Sheehan-Wells property, a parcel of land between Union and Lincoln Avenues, and creates new auto-entrance and parking lot.

One of the most infamous defeats in horse-racing history, Man O'War loses to Upset at Saratoga. The only loss of his 21 starts.

1937

New Betting Ring opens, extending from rear of Grandstand, designed by Albany architect Marcus T. Reynolds. Introduces new architectural vocabulary to Race Course of white cast iron shaped into playful equine motifs.

1943-5

Track closed due to World War II restrictions. Saratoga meeting held at Belmont Park.

1934

1892 Betting Ring extended.

1940

Pari-mutuel machines arrive at Saratoga Race Course. Almost 300 betting and cashing windows installed.

1928

New Clubhouse built in place of 1892 structure, designed by Samuel Adams Clark.

1936

Field Stand demolished and replaced with larger, steel stand.

1939

Saratoga Association acquires 5.9 acre plot from Fasig-Tipton Co.

New York State legalizes pari-mutuel wagering.

1945

Completion of additional extension to new Betting Ring, designed by architect Kenneth Reynolds. Linked Betting Ring with the Clubhouse.

In the ensuing chapters, these buildings and landscapes will be brought to life. This book charts the story of the design of the Spa's hallowed track, tracing its course over more than a century and a half of evolution. From a modest beginning in 1847, the tale is anchored by a succession of defining eras and individuals: the 1860s establishment of the thoroughbred track only a month after the Battle of Gettysburg by an Irish prize-fighter named John Morrissey; the leadership of Gottfried Walbaum, a notorious bookmaker whose infamy brought the track to its lowest ebb in the 1890s; the Gilded Age of the Race Course following a takeover by the far more respectable traction magnate and politician, William C. Whitney in 1901; and the formation and proprietorship of the New York Racing Association from 1955 to the present day. The racetrack's stands, stables and horticulture are unique memorials to the colorful personalities and politics that shaped the historic grounds. And moreover, they are palpable evidence of Saratoga's great design inheritance. Saratoga's tapestry of buildings, landscapes and vistas is a multi-layered chronicle of sporting, architectural and national history, the like of which no other racetrack in the world can boast.

Figure 2. The hippodrome at Jerash in Jordan (2nd century AD), typifies the formula of the Roman hippodromes.

CHAPTER ONE
BACKGROUND

No one can say with any certainty when horse racing first started, but surely as long as there have been people and horses, horses have raced. Horse racing ranks amongst the most ancient of sports. From the days of nomadic tribesmen racing the earliest domesticated horses across the plains of central Asia, pitting the speed and endurance of horses has gripped the imagination of mankind. By 648 BC mounted horse racing held in hippodromes had established itself on the schedule of the Olympic games, while Plato tells of a horseback race to venerate the Thracian goddess Bendis. Under the Roman Empire, equestrianism became a passion. It was under the Romans that the hippodrome became a recognizable building type. Typically, tiers of stone seating surrounded the racing field, at the far end of which were located the starting gates, sometimes lavishly decorated with mosaics and sculptures (Figure 2). Horse and chariot racing was the mass entertainment form of the era and the Romans carried with them an appetite for horse sports to the lands they conquered. In all probability, it was the Romans who established the pastime in Britain, the country long credited with fathering the modern sport of thoroughbred

When British colonialists arrived in America they brought their horses with them and immediately, horse racing began here too.

racing. Racing was established in Britain by the Middle Ages. In the twelfth century, horse races are recorded as having taken place on public holidays and by the sixteenth century, they were regular events, typically accompanying local fairs. It was in the seventeenth century though that the roots of modern, organized horse racing first took hold, under the fashionable impetus of the Stuart kings. James I, his son Charles I and grandson Charles II sparked a new aristocratic zeal for racing in the British Isles and under their patronage was established the royal course of Newmarket, ever since the unchallenged headquarters of racing the world across. With the monarchy acting as a driving force, the seventeenth century was a century of firsts for thoroughbred racing: the first stakes race was run; breeding practices were regulated; and a parliamentary act was initiated to conduct racing under written rules.

Yet there was no such standardization when it came to the courses themselves. British courses were typically established on country estates or on common ground alongside market towns, and were laid out to match the size and topography of the land upon a natural grass surface. From ovals to triangles, and pear shapes to figures of eight, the track layouts abounded in eccentricity *(Figure 3)*. The ground could be emphatically flat or steeply inclined, or somewhere in between. Always, though, were British races run on grass. By the opening of the eighteenth century, race meetings were prospering up and down the country.

When British colonialists arrived in America they brought their horses with them and immediately, horse racing began here too. British officials, loath to forego their fashionable gentlemanly sports, and large landowners with ample wealth and leisure time established the sport in America. However, no sooner had the sport been imported than it began to look very different to its British parent. America was yet an untamed country, thick with dense forests that could only be cleared with backbreaking toil and at tremendous cost. The young (and hungry) nation needed every inch of cleared land for agriculture and recreating the park-like courses of Britain with their meandering turf tracks was simply impractical. Instead, from the outset racing took a distinctly American format – horses and their riders made short, straight charges along village streets, narrow woodland paths, or whatever open space was available to them. Whereas British racing was conducted over long distances as a test of strength and stamina, American racing was a matter of agile startings and breakneck sprints.[3]

Racing was as yet ad hoc and unplanned, but it flourished in the Southern colonies where the "Cavalier Colonialists" engendered a passion for turf sports. The cleared tobacco fields of Virginia made the perfect setting for trials of speed. The circular or elliptical shape of these impromptu tracks – or so-called racefields – gave a foretaste of what was later to become the standard oval track format, so widely different to the British progenitors. The best jockeys were so synonymous with the state that they were known simply as "Virginia boys". Maryland had its

Ascot

Epsom

Goodwood

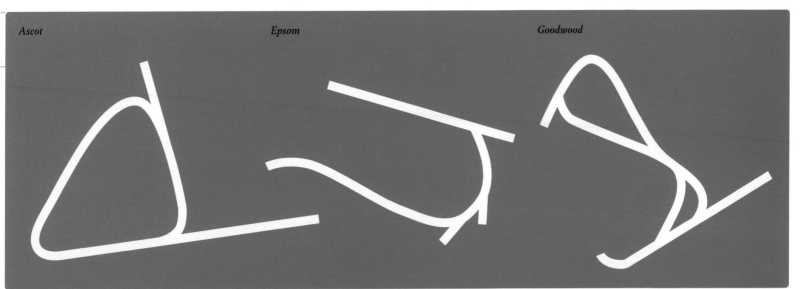

Saratoga

Keeneland

Churchill Downs

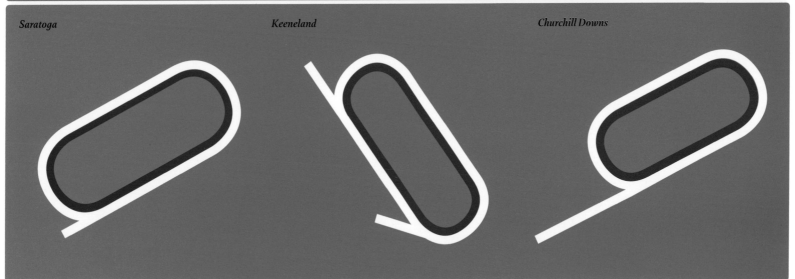

own jockey club by 1743, while, despite having a population of less than 15,000, the District of Columbia too had founded a jockey club by 1798.[4]

It was, however, in the North, that the country's first regular racetrack was laid out. Concerned about the dearth of good horses, in 1665 Richard Nicholls, the British governor of the New York colony, built a large, oval turf track on the open flatlands of Long Island known as Hempstead Plain (present-day Jamaica). Christened Newmarket, for over 100 years all New York society, from governors, to gentry to farmers, flocked to this track.[5] It gave rise to many imitators. The tracks of the Northern colonies were, typically, a mile around, with a grass surface marked out by poles. It was not until the opening of the celebrated Union Course in Long Island in 1819 that dirt tracks began to be popular (Figure 4). Contemporary commentator Cadwallader R. Colden observed that "the same horses take from three to five seconds more time to run a mile over the New Market turf than over the naked soil of the Union Course". Yielding faster racing, Union Course's "skinned" surface served as a new model for the country's tracks. Another first was also seen at

Union – it was the earliest course to be entirely surrounded by railings. Watching from carriages or upon horseback (there were no such luxuries as grandstands yet), racegoers gathered in their thousands at Union to watch some of racing history's most stirring and bitter contests. Not least of these was the North–South contest, opening on May 23, 1823. North Carolinian William Ransom Johnson – known as the "Napoleon of the Turf" – had challenged Yankee industrialist Cornelius Van Ranst to pit his racehorse, American Eclipse, against Johnson's five-year-old Sir Henry. American Eclipse, considered by Northerners to be the fastest horse in America, had been the focus of Southern resentment since he had beaten Sir Charles, "the lion of the Virginia turf", a year earlier. The match sparked a sporting frenzy. Astronomical sums were bet and up to 20,000 Southerners and 40,000 Northerners clamored to watch what was, in effect, America's first national sports event.[6]

Clearly, there was money to be made from the frenzy surrounding turf sports in these years. It was an opportunity that did not go unrecognized by a select band of enterprising residents in the small New York village of Saratoga Springs.

Figure 5. Bains de Saratoga, c1829.

CHAPTER TWO

SARATOGA SPRINGS AND ITS EARLIEST RACETRACK

When a young and ambitious lumberman named Gideon Putnam built a three-story tavern opposite a local mineral spring in a frontier New York hamlet at the opening of the nineteenth century, his neighbors ridiculed the undertaking; "Putnam's Folly", they nicknamed it. But, by the close of the century, when the Folly had become renowned the continent over as the centerpiece of the nation's most successful spa resort, it was Putnam who had the last laugh. The hamlet was, of course, Saratoga Springs, in the foothills of the Adirondacks and less than 30 miles north from the state capital, Albany. Long before Putnam arrived on the scene, the gently rolling terrain, thickly set with forests and natural springs, of Saratoga County had been home to native Iroquois. Countless generations of Iroquois had been drawn to the springs, bubbling with rich mineral water, for their curative powers. Nevertheless, it was not until the second half of the eighteenth century that European settlers discovered the secret. In 1771 the Superintendent of Indian Affairs for the British colonies, Sir William Johnson, was taken by the Iroquois to sample the healing waters of a spring dubbed High Rock. Johnson, who had been regularly plagued by an old war wound, marveled at its restorative properties. In little time word spread, and around High Rock the village of Saratoga Springs took root.

Following the arrival of the quick-witted Putnam in 1789, the potential of Saratoga's precious natural resource was seized. With his own tavern – later renamed the Union Hotel – as a nucleus, Putnam created a spa resort. He excavated, tubed and promoted numerous springs; donated land for a church, school and cemetery; laid out the elm-bordered avenue today known as Broadway; and, as visitor numbers grew, began construction of a second hotel, Congress Hall, in 1811. Saratoga's waters were lauded as a cure-all, treating everything and anything from gout to ulcers to obesity. Given the treatments found on an average nineteenth-century prescription – bloodletting, purging, opium – it hardly seems surprising that invalids flocked to the Springs.[7] Soon, though, the resort's health benefits subsided next to the pursuit of pleasure, and Putnam's town became the hub of America's tourist industry.

Alongside nearby Ballston, Saratoga Springs was the first national resort *(Figure 5)*.[8] Pleasure-

Given the treatments found on an average 19th-century prescription – bloodletting, purging, opium – it hardly seems surprising that invalids flocked to the Springs.

seekers from across the land were drawn to its hotels and boarding houses, where friends, business associates and strangers alike entered into its round of dancing, banquets and games. In summer 1818, a record number of 4,200 visitors flocked to the town's numerous hotels, and this figure soared after 1832 when the new railroad connection vastly improved journey times and comfort. In 1833, its permanent population of 2,000 swelled with an intake of 8,000 summertime visitors.[9] By the 1830s, Saratoga reigned as the queen of the nation's resorts. "All the world is here," enthused Philip Hone in his diary in 1839,

"politicians and dandies; cabinet ministers and ministers of the gospel; office-holders and office seekers; humbuggers and humbugged; fortune hunters and hunters of woodcock; anxious mothers and lovely daughters."[10] It was in the early or mid-1830s that the first public opportunities for gambling were established. Faro, chuck-a-luck and roulette went on in billiard halls and bowling alleys, while the first house purely devoted to gambling opened in 1842 in an alley near the United States Hotel. The *New York Herald* wrote in 1847 that,

At Saratoga the pulpit and the gaming table appear to monopolize everything. Every day at dinner the highest dignitaries of the church are to be found sitting side by side, in pleasant social communication with the gamblers of Park Row. A pious father of the Protestant Episcopal church addresses in the blandest accent, a notorious faro-table keeper: "My dear sir allow me to help you to a piece of this chicken."[11]

With its lively and unorthodox lifestyle, Saratoga Springs was from its earliest days marked by this intertwining of tourism and gaming. Its status as a gambling haven placed an almost indelible stamp on the townscape that soon overshadowed the appeal of the Spa's waters.

Figure 6. A scene from the 1853 Saratoga New York State Fair gives an impression of what the 1847 fair would have looked like.

Saratoga's first racetrack, the Saratoga Trotting Course, emerged from the glint of this gambling flame. Impromptu sprints were held on the streets of the village, with horses and their riders hurtling along its thoroughfares at such headlong speeds that the town officially banned the activity in 1825. The idea of organized racing was first kindled as early as the mid-1820s, when "sundry inhabitants" approached the state Assembly for permission to build a racetrack. The idea came to nothing – until, that is, the 1840s, the decade when racing got underway in the Springs. Racing had not in fact been legal in New York since 1802 when Puritan leaders had succeeded in outlawing "all racing and running, pacing or trotting of horses, mares, geldings, for any bet or stakes, in money, goods or chattels, or other valuable thing". But, state fairs provided a perfect foil for conducting the activity in all but name. By the mid-nineteenth century, it was clear that harness racing was a much-loved and tremendously successful component of the county agricultural fairs and a loophole had to be found to dodge the irksome anti-racing law. Thus, "horse races" became "trials of speed" and "exhibitions of horses" – an ideal camouflage for illegal racing which Saratoga was soon to capitalize upon.[12]

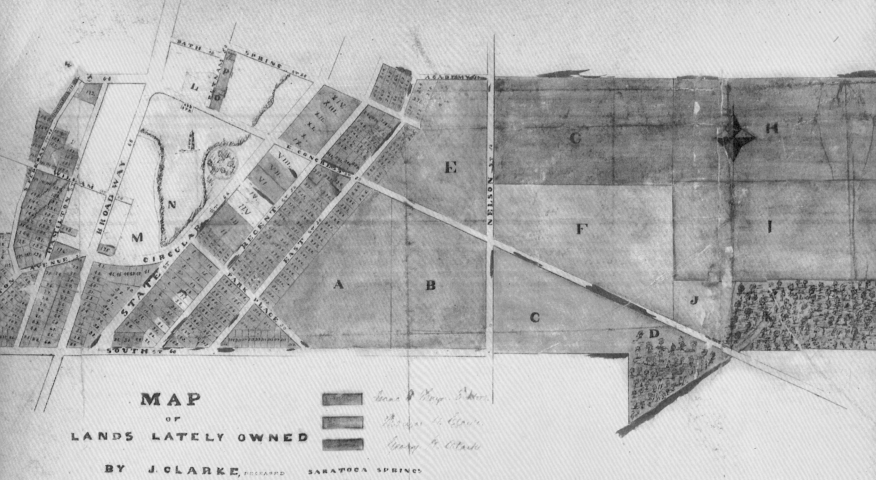

MAP

OF

LANDS LATELY OWNED

BY J. CLARKE, DECEASED. SARATOGA SPRINGS

Figure 7. Map of the Lands Lately Owned by J. Clarke, 1851. The Race Course is probably today sited on the land segments marked C and F.

Figure 8. Barn #76, Horse Haven. The barn's Greek Revival cornice suggests it pre-dates the 1847 trotting track.

The New York State Fair came to Saratoga in September 1847 and with it came a flurry of building activity, preparing a complex just east of the village boundary to host the fair's visitors and breadth of displays *(Figure 6)*. Meanwhile, on a nearby patch of land local impresarios Alfonso Patten and James M. Cole, funded by James Marvin, began developing a new trotting course. Its site is well known today as the location of the present-day Horse Haven. Evidence suggests that the stretch of land was owned by one Dr John Clarke, and, after his death in 1846, passed to his sons George and Thomas Clarke *(Figure 7)*. The English-born John Clarke ranked amongst Saratoga's most celebrated businessmen. Creating the nucleus of present-day Congress Park, Clarke monopolized the town's natural resource of spring waters. He made his fortune by establishing the Congress Spring Water Company, the profits of which no doubt enabled him to purchase the entire south-east quadrant of the village from the early- to mid- nineteenth century (including a large proportion of what constitutes the twenty-first-century Race Course property).

Patten and Cole were an unlikely pairing to run a racetrack – the former was a liverykeeper whilst the latter was a butcher – yet on August 14, 1847 racing commenced there to a crowd of 5,000. This was, in fact, a whole month before the State Fair opened, quashing any credence to the pretence that this was a fair exhibition. Officials washed their hands of any responsibility for its legality, arguing it was outside the fairgrounds complex and beyond the village line. Gambling contributed too much to the resort's success for local authorities to do much but turn a blind eye. More race meetings were advertised within the fair's program, including a race for "running horses" – the first official thoroughbred race to take place at Saratoga.[13]

The oval track was laid out seven furlongs in length (7/8 mile) and about 60 feet wide on an even stretch of land.[14] Carriages lined up along its straight, two deep on opening day. One dollar gave admittance to the grandstand, while a seat in a lower stand, seemingly in the infield, cost 50 cents.[15] Little else is known of the stands of Saratoga's first racetrack. While the *New York Herald* sneered that "such an establishment is not much of a recommendation for the morals of a neighborhood" (August 10, 1847), the trotting course was largely enthusiastically received. "Messrs. Patten and Cole have fitted up a very fine trotting course," remarked the *Saratoga Republican*, "admirably adapted to the issue to which it is applied" (August 9, 1847). The *Spirit of the Times* described the course as "a very pretty one...the Stands are good, and the Proprietors, Messrs. Patten and Cole, civil and obliging" (October 9, 1847). In truth though, the course was narrow, covered with "piny growths" and with a grandstand far too small to hold the ardent spectators. Nevertheless, for sixteen years it served as the popular staging ground for Saratoga's trotting races.

While no trace of the public stands remain, it is very probable that several buildings still standing at Horse Haven date from this early ownership. The icehouse and farmhouse in Campfire Court and a large barn (numbered as barn #76) within the infield of Horse Haven's track share Greek Revival detailing which was typical of pre-1850 domestic construction. Together they may have constituted part of an earlier farm complex dating to John Clarke's ownership. The barn was built as a two-story structure *(Figure 8)*. Its horizontal clapboard and board-and-batten facades and slate roofs are characteristic of Horse Haven's nineteenth-century buildings. But its prominent cornice is symptomatic

Figure 9. Ice House, Horse Haven. The building's corner pilasters and prominent cornice exemplified the trend for Greek Revival in the first half of the 19th century.

of the popularity of Greek Revival architecture from the 1820s to 1850, and provided a mark of distinction to a normally humble building type. The same is true of the icehouse *(Figure 9)*. Otherwise a very simple building, the icehouse was ennobled by neo-Grecian detailing, such as its bold pediment, cornice and corner pilasters.

Following the inauguration of Horse Haven as an organized racetrack in 1847, these early farmstead buildings were joined by others. As the racing venture prospered, scattered groupings of stable and kitchen buildings appeared on the infield in increasing numbers. Dating most probably to the late 1840s, 1850s and early 1860s, and located in the areas now known as Campfire Court and West Horse Haven, these buildings are as much a part of the Saratoga season today as they were in the days of Patten and Cole. Although differing widely in

Figure 10. Campfire Court, Horse Haven. Some of the earliest barns on the Race Course property, built to house the trotters of Saratoga's trotting track, opened in 1847.

for example, were sited on the wall opposite the door to facilitate cross-ventilation, which all such literature insisted upon as the stable builder's chief priority.[16] Each stall was enclosed by a hinged dutch door – a style of door separated into top and bottom halves introduced by Dutch colonists settling into the Hudson River Valley in the seventeenth century – with iron latches and strap hinges. Their uniform gray and beige color made for a marked identity, contrasting with the sharp white and green coloration of twentieth-century backstretch construction. In broad terms, all Saratoga's stables conform to one of nine architectural typologies, and the formula seen here is the most prevalent of all, defining all pre-1900 examples after racing was introduced to the site. The layout of Campfire Court and West Horse Haven is, though, idiosyncratic. Their barns are clustered in loose, seemingly haphazard groups of three or four with the effect of forming interior courts, perhaps consciously devised to create walking areas for the horses.[17]

For 16 summers, the oval track and Campfire Court and West Horse Haven barns were the setting of Saratoga's trotting races. Soon though, thanks to the vision of an unlikely entrepreneur, an Irish pugilist, burglar and Tammany Hall racketeer known as Old Smoke, racing operations at the Spa stepped up a gear. The physical fabric of Saratoga's racetrack was about to burgeon as racing operations entered a dynamic new era.

sizes and orientation, the stables were built to a basic formula *(Figure 10)*. They reached a height of one-and-a-half stories, with single-loaded stalls below a half-story loft space accessed via the gable ends. In all likelihood, the loft spaces of the stables acted as temporary accommodation, accessed by the wall ladders that remain today. Whereas now, Saratoga's backstretch acreage is cast with bunkhouses to quarter its summer community of stable hands, the

evidence of nineteenth- and early twentieth-century maps indicates that no stand-alone dwellings were provided at this point. The wooden-frame structures were roofed with slate with an overhanging front shed row, supported upon robust timber posts. To a great degree the fabric of the West Horse Haven and Campfire Court stables conformed closely to the prescriptions of mid-nineteenth-century treatises on barn construction. The stable windows,

Figure 11. "First Meeting of the Season of the Saratoga Association", Frank Leslie's Illustrated Newspaper, August 16, 1879.

CHAPTER THREE
OLD SMOKE

In 1863, bitter civil war was consuming the nation; struggle and suffering subjugated the population. Yet, on August 3 of that year, a new era dawned for Saratoga. On what the *Saratogian* described as a "shimmering summer day", thousands gathered to watch Lizzie W., a three-year-old filly, beat the colt Captain Moore to the post in the first race of an experimental meeting of thoroughbred running races,

launching a tradition that survives to this day. There were only eight races in the meeting, held at what had hitherto been the Trotting Course, but the town of Saratoga Springs was never to be the same again.

The 1863 meeting was the brainchild of one of the biggest, if not *the* biggest, personalities in American gambling history – John Morrissey *(Figure 12)*. With "sledgehammer fists", a ruthless ambition

and visionary ingenuity, Morrissey propelled himself from an impoverished childhood as an illiterate Irish immigrant, to become the nation's first sporting hero, a New York gambling tycoon, and an influential politician. The Morrissey family emigrated to Troy, New York, circa 1834, where John quickly gained a reputation as an unsavory troublemaker. By the time he was 18, Morrissey had

Figure 12. John Morrissey, the prize-fighting, Irish immigrant was the unlikely founder of Saratoga's first thoroughbred racetrack.

been indicted for burglary, assault and battery, and assault with intent to kill.[18] Uprooting temporarily to California, he there acquired a flair for gambling and bare-knuckle prize fighting. In 1853 he settled back East, moving to New York City. There he thrust his way to claim the title of the American boxing championship – one of the "bloodiest battles ever fought on the American continent" – and to a place in the seedy world of New York politics. His exploits there were the stuff of lore and legend. He acquired an idiosyncratic nickname during a brawl over a prostitute in which he was knocked onto a spilled bed of hot coals. The smell of burning flesh filled the room. Bystanders showered the singed Morrissey with cold water, and the scorching, blinding steam that exuded unbalanced his opponent and gave the Irishman the opportunity he needed. Morrissey kept swinging and knocked out his adversary. From then on, he was known as Old Smoke.[19] His alliance with the Tammany Hall Democrats meant that the authorities turned a blind eye when he opened a string of gambling houses in Manhattan. And in 1861 he turned his attention to the fashionable resort of Saratoga Springs. That year, he expanded his gambling empire with the opening of a house

on Matilda Street (now Woodlawn Avenue), which was followed several years later by the Club House Casino – Morrissey's "great gilded gambling palace" – in Congress Park frequented by the great and the good such as Ulysses S. Grant, John D. Rockefeller and Mark Twain.

The quick-witted Irishman spotted another profit-making opportunity in the resort town. In 1863 Morrissey seized upon Saratoga's background in high-profile trotting races to organize the now-legendary four-day thoroughbred meeting at Patten and Cole's trotting track. While the grisly civil war raged on, welcome relief from the wartime news came in the form of Morrissey's newspaper advertisements for a series of thoroughbred races to take place in August. The *Daily Saratogian* announcement read, "Running Races! AT SARATOGA!...All sections of the North and West, and some portions of the South will be represented by their best horses...Excellent racing is anticipated. John Morrissey, Proprietor". Morrissey's ambitions seemed to transcend even the bitter North-South conflict.[20] With a little help from some well-to-do and powerful associates, such as Cornelius Vanderbilt, William R. Travers, and Leonard Jerome,

Figure 13. Saratoga Race Course, 1888. Print of the 1864 circuit, showing the Grandstand (on right), public stand (on left) and Horse Haven beyond.

Morrissey leased the land and put up a $2,700 purse to stage Saratoga's first season of thoroughbred running races.

That inaugural meeting drew 27 horses and 15,000 people, each paying $1 for an admission card. However, the modest 1840s grandstand was no longer standing and the erstwhile trotting track had no building to accommodate them. Moreover good views of the track were scarce through the assortment of barns and pine trees on the site. In terms of the track itself, its turns were precariously tight.[21] Nevertheless, these shortcomings clearly

mattered little to Saratoga's early turfites for overnight the resort became summer's horse-racing capital. The town hotels were full to capacity – on the final day of racing, guest numbers totaled 25 per cent more than the peak of the 1862 season. Organized betting (although still prohibited) was installed in the United States Hotel. To the *Spirit of the Times*, it was a "great success". Morrissey, it commended, had "secured a fine sport". Society had clearly been bitten by the racing bug.

Reveling in the meeting's social and financial success, on the day after the last race Morrissey

drew together a band of society magnates and turf enthusiasts to found a jockey club, the Saratoga Association. Over $20,000 was almost immediately subscribed, and a new track was summarily planned. For this, 71 acres on the south side of East Congress Street (now Union Avenue) were purchased for $7,108.75 and added to the original Trotting Course property of 23 acres, which was to be retained as a training ground.[22] William R. Travers, a stockbroker, was declared president of the fledgling association, with his business partner Leonard Jerome and John Purdy, a wine merchant and gentleman jockey, both

Figure 15. *"The Races at Saratoga". This Harper's Weekly illustration (August 24, 1867) shows a crowded Grandstand and the two judges' stands.*

Figure 16. Grandstand, Hamilton Racecourse, Australia, c1873. Its decorative cast iron and fanciful turrets contrast with Saratoga's plain timber stand.

Figure 14. The august, classical entrance to the 1864 Race Course, through which can be seen the Grandstand with its long colonnade of arches.

acting as his deputies. Morrissey's name, however, was nowhere to be found. Although by all accounts he probably provided the majority of the capital, his scandalous reputation made polite society uneasy. While he played an essential role in the enterprise until his death in 1878, his name was conveniently absent from the Association's list of directors. The Saratoga Association's executive committee had a

distinctive constitution. Overwhelmingly, it was formed of men of business, men like Travers, Jerome, Erastus Corning and James Marvin. And they brought a business-minded ethic to racing operations at the Spa. Gone was the unplanned, local character of match-racing; horse racing became organized. It became a regularly-programmed sport on a national scale, and it was governed by a tight circle of an elite group of men.[23] Jerome was to emerge as the United States' most successful racetrack entrepreneur, building Jerome Park, Morris Park and Sheepshead Bay and co-founding the American Jockey Club. Travers was one of Sheepshead Bay's financiers and a partner in Annieswood Stable, one of the most successful stables in the country. Managing the Saratoga facility was Charles Wheatley, who had served as the secretary of the Kentucky Association and ran its Lexington track, and was later the engineer for the Jerome Park track.

The Saratoga Association's new course opened on August 2, 1864 for a 5 day summer meeting.[24] Its opening was a landmark day in national sporting history – the track was the United States' first modern sports facility and one which continues today as the oldest extant example in the country.

And, judging from the commendations of the press, it was an uncontested hit. The *Republican and Sentinel* dubbed the track "the best in the country"; the *Saratogian* eulogized that the "splendid" new course was "much admired by all who visit it".

Under the professional guidance of Wheatley, local engineer Charles H. Ballard was responsible for the mile-long track *(Figure 13)*. It had a diagonal chute to accommodate a range of starts and measured 43 feet in width (rising to 63 feet on the home stretch). No physical trace remains of the track or buildings today, but contemporary photographs and press reports allow us to picture for ourselves the complex that the early racegoers would have encountered. Their first sight would have been that of a neo-classical gateway *(Figure 14)*. Standing at the intersection of Lincoln and Union Avenues, the stucco-clad masonry gate made for a simple, yet imposing entrance. Consisting of a double ingress, its heavy entablature carried a shallow pediment capped by urns. A sinewing pathway, lined with newly-planted trees, led from it to the rear of the Grandstand. Upon opening day, carriage after carriage traveled through this gate and deposited Saratoga's fashionable pleasure seekers on

Figure 17. Saratoga's Grandstand. Note the uncovered public stand to the left.

the six-acre open stretch of land alongside the track. Another six-acre tract, shaded by pine trees, was reserved as a cooling area for the horses.

Along the west side of the track, a Grandstand was erected and, unlike its predecessor at the Horse Haven track, we know something of it through contemporary illustrations and press commentaries:

The main building is two hundred feet long, by thirty wide... On the lower floor are reception rooms, saloons, halls, &c., with a colonnade in front the entire length of the building. From each end of this colonnade, stairways rise to the gallery above. There are also four other stairways on the side of the stand next to the track. It is estimated that the gallery will seat about 2,000 persons.[25]

It was a simple, timber building, architecturally modest but functionally appropriate *(Figure 15)*. According to the *Saratogian,* the new Grandstand made ample provision for the eager attendees, "affording a perfect view of the entire course from each seat".[26] Raked seating for spectators was provided

beneath a slate gable roof carried upon a timber frame of unadorned trusses and posts. Beneath the tiered seating, the first floor of the building held "retiring and refreshment rooms, ladies boudoirs and every needful convenience".[27] A colonnade of tall, round arches which ran along the length of the rear of the stand gave access to these spaces. No surviving records name its designer or builder.

In style, the Grandstand was a modest example of Carpenter Gothic. This eclectic architectural mode was a curious nineteenth-century hybrid unique to the United States, characterized by the application of scrolled ornaments, pointed gables, board-and-batten cladding, "gingerbread" trim, and other exaggerated surface motifs to functionally simple wooden buildings and was kindled by the designs of landscape architect Andrew Jackson Downing. Saratoga's Grandstand was an understated case of the Carpenter Gothic – which frequently inclined to the flamboyant, even fantastical – but its carved bargeboards, trefoil-shaped "gingerbread" cut-outs on its gable ends, and wooden board-and-batten walls were illustrative of the style. Its wooden frame was also typical of the style and of the era. Not only was wood in plentiful supply in the Adirondack foothills, but it was a far less expensive option than brick or stone and easily worked with the new generation of steam-powered scroll saws and treadle jigsaws.

By the time that Saratoga's Grandstand was built, grandstands had emerged as a distinctive building type in their own right. A standardized architectural format had been developed in Britain in the second half of the eighteenth century, beginning with the grandstand designed by celebrated architect John Carr at York Racecourse in the 1750s. By the mid-nineteenth century, grandstands at racetracks across the world shared a basic vocabulary of tiered cross-section with raked seating above and enclosed refreshment and social spaces below, as seen at Longchamp in Paris (1854), New York's Jerome Park (1866) and Hamilton Racecourse in Australia (1873). Morrissey's Grandstand shared this format. "[I]t will compare favorably with many of the most famous in Europe," boasted the *New York Times* ahead of its opening (June 19, 1864). Yet in terms of its architectural pretensions, the Saratoga complex was notably plainer than the typical European and Australian examples. In this it exemplified the buildings of North American tracks as a whole. Whilst in Europe and Australia, the construction materials of choice were largely brick, stone and

Figure 19. Barn #37, Elm Court. View along the shed row.

iron, American grandstands tended to be timber structures with a far greater emphasis on utility than architectural fashions. The diminutive grandstand of Hamilton Racecourse, for instance, built less than a decade later than Saratoga's illustrates these differences *(Figure 16)*. Its elaborate double-curve corrugated iron roof was supported on cast-iron columns and iron trusses. The cast iron lace balustrade and octagonal turrets were a model of the Victorian taste for ornate decoration.

Nonetheless, the new Race Course fanned a fervor in the village. "Neither pains nor expense have been spared to render it perfect in all departments," rhapsodized one commentator. It was "a model institution", he continued.[28] The complex was completed by an open Betting Ring, immediately east of the Grandstand, and two judges' stands overlooking the finishing line. These small, pavilion-like buildings were wooden polygonals with pitched roofs. The officials, raised aloft upon a dais, stood

behind wooden railings as they presided over the action on the track.

The success of the 1864 meeting was eclipsed by that of 1865. Every hotel, every boarding house, and almost every private residence, wrote the *New York Times*, was full to bursting as visitors swarmed to Saratoga Springs like bees in a hive in anticipation of the annual racing carnival. The length of the meeting was increased to six days while the size of the Grandstand grew likewise. The 1864 structure was extended to the east and west by over half its length to some 320 feet, providing a total of 4,500 "elegantly cushioned" seats for the assemblage of beauty, wealth and fashion vying for a spot in the stand. In time for the meeting, an additional stand was erected near the clubhouse turn (first turn). Smaller and more modestly appointed than the Grandstand, this "field" or "public" stand was originally uncovered *(Figure 17)*. By 1875, though, it had acquired a roof, giving it a silhouette broadly similar to the Grandstand, even down to its trefoil gable windows.

1865 was a landmark year in another respect – it was in that year that Saratoga's racing became legal in the eyes of the law. The 1802 anti-betting state legislation had not been repealed, but a little-known bill passed in 1854 sanctioned racing that was conducted for "improving the breed of horses". To the Saratoga Association, this provided the perfect loophole to make its racing activities legal. In 1865, the corporation was reborn as the Saratoga

Figure 20. Barn #61, East Horse Haven. The hinged dutch doors, board-and-batten walls and wall ladders leading up to the half-story loft are typical of Saratoga's 19th-century stables.

Association for the Improvement of the Breed of Horses. Under provision five, its charter stated,

The objects of said association shall be to improve the breed of horses; and for the carrying out the objects of this act, the association may hold one or more meetings upon their grounds in each year, for the exhibition and trial of such animals as the directors may deem proper; and may offer and give such premiums as they may agree upon, for the superiority in the object sought for.[29]

The Association's new course stripped Horse Haven of its original function as a racing circuit, yet it continued to play a chief role in racing operations both for the stabling and training of thoroughbreds. As racing in Saratoga grew in popularity and the Saratoga Association increased in confidence, more and more stable accommodation rose in Horse Haven's oval infield and on the surrounding land, clustered in two areas known as Elm Court and East Horse Haven. "In the training track grounds the two new stables are nearly finished," announced the Saratogian in July 1869, "while the other stables are fast filling up with crack nags." It was in the ensuing years that the old trotting track began to earn its reputation as a bucolic retreat for horses, shaded by a growing canopy of pines, spruces and cedars. Krick's 1880 *Guide to the Turf* reported that

The club is amply provided with stable accommodations, a majority of which are, however, in a pine grove known as the "old track", where the air is cool and salubrious, that horses recover from the effects of hard work sooner, and feel hard work less than at any Race Course in the eastern division of the country.

The ambience earned the ground its "haven" epithet, by which it had come to be known as by the 1880s.

In terms of design and construction, the Elm Court and East Horse Haven stables are more or less identical to the earlier stable structures within Campfire Court or West Horse Haven, taking the form of one-and-a-half story, single-loaded barns framed with heavy timber posts and beams, clad with board-and-batten sidings and roofed with slate *(Figures 18, 19, 20)*. However, with the new administration came a new approach to the organization of Horse Haven's barns. Contrasting with the informal layout of Campfire Court and West Horse Haven, the later nineteenth-century stables and kitchens were arranged in ordered, parallel rows with gables aligned. Processions of trees were planted, evenly-spaced, running alongside their lengths, and narrow, oval walking circuits inserted in between or around them *(Figure 21)*. This rational, uniform layout attests to the business-like spirit of organization, hitherto unknown, which the Saratoga Association brought to racing operations

Figure 21. East Horse Haven, an avenue of stables.

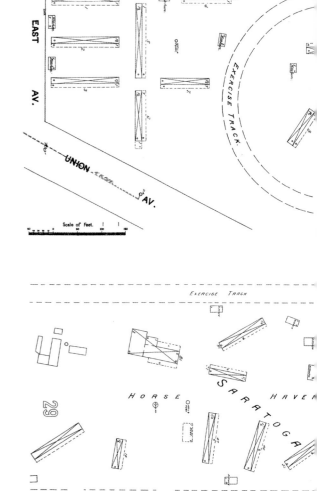

at the Spa. The sharp change in orientation is well illustrated by comparing East Horse Haven with the adjacent, earlier, West Horse Haven on the 1889 Sanborn Fire Insurance Maps *(Figure 22)*. This map is the earliest surviving plan of the land and its structures. The collection of Sanborn Maps, dating to 1889, 1895, 1900, 1932 and 1954, provide one of the most illuminating and invaluable guides we have to the changing character of the Race Course property. The labeled, bird's eye view of Horse Haven given in the 1889 map shows its infield covered with barns. By the time the next map was made in 1895 the tradition of naming pathways in Horse Haven for celebrated thoroughbreds had been set, with Procter Knot, Lamplighter, Kingston and Springbok Avenues clearly marked *(Figure 23)*.[30]

Whilst only photographs remain of Morrissey's Grandstand and public stand, the stables that were built under his management are extant today and still play host to would-be winners every summer. Their amazing survival is testament to their quality of craftsmanship and design, and a visual memento of this epochal chapter in Saratoga's long lifetime. As the nineteenth century entered its last decades though, a new chapter was to begin, and it changed the architectural character of the Race Course forever.

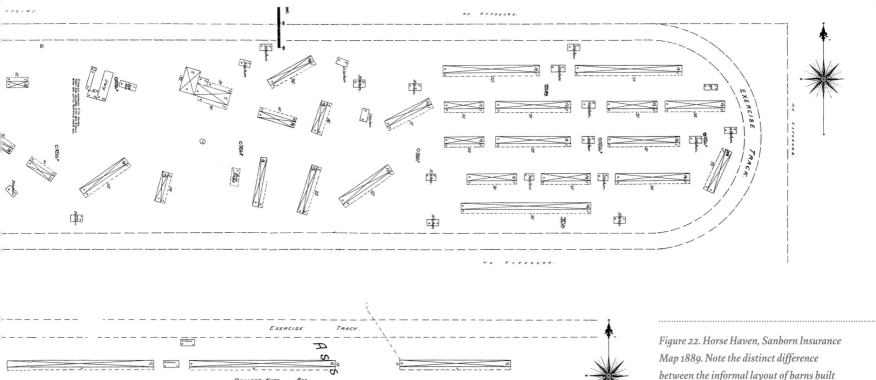

Figure 22. Horse Haven, Sanborn Insurance Map 1889. Note the distinct difference between the informal layout of barns built during the days of the trotting track and the parallel and perpendicular rows of stabling built by the Saratoga Association.

Figure 23. Horse Haven, Sanborn Insurance Map 1895. By the late 19th century, the tradition of naming Horse Haven's walkways after champion thoroughbreds was set.

Figure 24. Saratoga Race Course's brand new Frontside complex opened in time for the 1892 summer season.

CHAPTER FOUR
THE WICKEDEST SUMMER RESORT

An era came to an end on May 1, 1878, when John "Old Smoke" Morrissey breathed his last. Fifteen thousand mourners and 50 carriages followed the poor son of Tipperary to his grave in Troy, New York. But turf fever in Saratoga was in no way abated. Indeed, countrywide the sport was booming in the 1870s and 1880s. The Preakness Stakes was first run in 1873 at Pimlico, and the Kentucky Derby had its inaugural run in 1875 at Churchill Downs. Congress even adjourned for a day in 1877 to attend a meeting at Pimlico. The mania spread westwards too, as meetings in California, Ohio, Illinois and Indiana were publicized in eastern seaboard turf journals. Saratoga, though, stood out from the crowd. With an ethic that emphasized "sports for sport's sake", it drew the best stables and most illustrious racegoers. The post-war economy had bred a new generation of wealth. At the midpoint of the century, the whole country could only boast some 20 millionaires, but by 1890 this figure had multiplied to 4,000 – and Saratoga welcomed them with open arms. Tammany sachems, newly-enriched carpetbaggers, financiers and railroad magnates all beat a path to Saratoga in August.

At the midpoint of the century, the whole country could only boast some 20 millionaires, but by 1890 this figure had multiplied to 4,000 – and Saratoga welcomed them with open arms.

After the death of Morrissey, however, the Race Course's luster slowly began to fade and the track entered an unsettled period. Its lease and management was taken on by Charles Reed and Albert Spencer.[31] Since the latter years of the Civil War, Reed and Spencer had moved in prominent gambling circles of New York City, where, as part of a syndicate, they operated two highly profitable gaming houses. Reed was an old-time Southern gambler, loud voiced and showily dressed, who had killed a man in New Orleans in 1862. Spencer, on the other hand, was reserved and serious with a passion for collecting art that set him apart from the average gaming-house proprietor of the time. They must have made for an odd pairing at Saratoga, but for several years it was nevertheless a fruitful one.[32] Saratoga's racing traditions and routines continued much as before under the duo, but their regime was not to last. "While the merry-go-round spun on, righteousness was seething in the wings."[33]

From the late 1870s, anti-gambling sentiment began to build in the United States. Whilst strictly illegal, in many states betting pools had persisted unchecked throughout the nineteenth century. However, in the last decades of the century the racing industry experienced the mounting pressure and wrath of social reformists and temperance leaders, while widespread whispering of fixed races served to fan the flames of public outrage. An 1886 visit from Anthony Comstock, the secretary of the New York Society for Suppression of Vice, to Saratoga led to 20 of its gaming houses temporarily closing down. His public vilification of gambling as "a disgrace and a detriment to the community's progress" incited a small yet rich group of locals to a sustained reform drive.[34] Beset by anti-gambling partisans and the rebuffs of Saratoga society, Reed withdrew from the track's ownership in 1887 leaving Spencer in sole control. It was a timely move on Reed's part, since from 1889 the track came

under fire from a moral crusader in the form of Wall Street extraordinaire Spencer Trask. With a vast fortune and a wide social web, Trask was a powerful man and he embarked upon a personal mission to remodel the resort town into an urbane playground resort for the wealthy. In his vision there was no room for the insidious evils of the racetrack. Hiring a band of private detectives, Trask built a body of evidence against Spencer's gaming operations and launched a vitriolic tirade against the track's illegal gambling in his newspaper, the *Saratoga Union*. The campaign was ill-received amongst Saratogians, but, in 1890, Spencer gave way to his pressure and announced his intention to renounce control of Saratoga Race Course.[35]

It was no simple matter to find a new management, however. Indeed, for a short time the track was blighted by successive transitions of ownership. Contemporary press reports shed light on this troubled time in the track's history and the

Figure 25. "Greetings from Saratoga". Inexpensive and convenient, hand-tinted postcards showcased the Springs' most famous sites and scenes, including its state-of-the-art Betting Ring, Grandstand and Clubhouse ensemble.

largely drawn from the ranks America's society set. Hearst (1820-1891) and Arkell (1856-1930) were both businessmen with no prior experience of running a racetrack. Hearst had amassed a mining fortune on the Pacific coast, before becoming a US senator and embarking upon the formation of a racing stable, largely to outdo his fellow businessman and rival Senator Leland Stanford, the founder of California's Stanford University. Arkell was a publisher, whose company produced a host of popular newspapers and magazines including *Judge, Frank Leslie's Illustrated Weekly* and *Demarest Magazine.* Wheatley, though, was a Race Course stalwart, having served as the Association's secretary for 26 years.

The takeover was greeted by a tide of optimism:

The new blood and new methods to be introduced by the new management are bound to tell, for this means more liberal stakes and purses and a complete change from the slipshod methods that have been in vogue. Senator Hearst and W. J. Arkell, who are the moving spirits in the new club, have plenty of wealth at command to make the new association play a more important part in racing than it ever has before.[36]

The *Sun* proclaimed that "the reorganized Saratoga Association, with new life and additional capital, announces the intention of taking a position second to none".[37] Moreover, this capital, it was reported, was going to be put to use in a splendid new building campaign. "The old racetrack is to be completely rebuilt in the modern style and with modern conveniences," wrote the *New York Times.*

narrow sphere of gambling and turf men that steered its course. Throughout 1889 and 1890, newspapers whispered of imminent sales and likely vendees. These rumours were ratified when on August 17, 1890 the *New York Times* definitively reported that "it is now known beyond question that the Saratoga race track has changed hands". Its new proprietors were then still a matter of speculation, but it was rumored that behind the transfer was a syndicate

of wealthy gentlemen including Pierre Lorillard, August Belmont Sr., John A. Morris, Senator George Hearst and A. J. Cassett, with publisher W. J. Arkell at the helm. By October 29, the same newspaper confirmed that the officials and trustees of the new Saratoga Association had been named, with Senator Hearst as president, Arkell as vice president, and Charles Wheatley as secretary. Its membership contained several competent turfmen but was

Figure 26. Racing, against the backdrop of the sloping peaks of the Grandstand's iconic roof.

"The intention of the new lessees being to make it one of the handsomest and complete tracks in the country."[38] The excitement surrounding the improvements spread across the nation; as far as even Minnesota the local press enthused that "no expense will be spared to make it thoroughly complete in every particular".[39]

The fervor, though, was premature. By April 10, 1891, The Sun carried the headline "Mr Albert Spencer Once More Owns the Saratoga Track". At the beginning of the year, Hearst had fallen dangerously ill and he died on February 28.[40] With one of the prime movers lost from the Association, the financial burden was too great and Arkell retired from racing entirely, even selling his own racehorses. The controlling interest in the track reverted back to the reluctant Spencer.[41] Nonetheless, the intended improvements were not, it appears, abandoned. Though "the elaborate plans of Senator Hearst will be abandoned, as it will require too much capital to carry them through to a successful issue," the *New York Times* relayed, Spencer "will, however, carry out in the main the plans which had been devised."[42]

Quickly, however, the track changed hands yet again, and onto the stage stepped Gottfried "Dutch Fred" Walbaum. In mid-August 1891 Walbaum had made an offer for the Saratoga Association on behalf of the Hudson County Jockey Club, of which he was president.[43] And by 1892 this ignominious figure of the New York underworld had majority control of the track, launching it into one of its darkest eras. The sweating, swearing Walbaum made his money, it was reported, running a brothel and a gambling house in the Bowery, an insalubrious neighborhood in southern Manhattan. With these ill-gotten gains, he purchased the Guttenberg track in New Jersey. Introducing effective administration and winter racing, Walbaum and the Hudson County Jockey Club transformed Guttenberg into a veritable goldmine. However, their questionable practices made the racing facility notorious, to the extent that the name Guttenberg became a "synonym for all the crookedness... in the horse-racing business". Rumors abounded that "owners experimented with electric batteries and narcotics while seeking to have their horses win races at good prices", while the results of many races were almost certainly known before they were run.[44] Bullheaded and brash, Walbaum yet exhibited a strange unworldliness in running his tracks. The "Dutch Book" was supposedly named in his honor. This is a book in which the odds have been figured so inconsistently that by betting on every horse the bettor is guaranteed to profit, no matter which horse wins.[45] Unsurprisingly, several eyebrows were raised when Dutch Fred arrived at Saratoga.

Figure 27. The Grandstand's pinnacled roofline is an unofficial emblem of the track.

His presence lingers on at Saratoga today, for it was under his leadership that the nucleus of the present Grandstand – with its sweeping slate roof and bouquet of pinnacles – was built. The Grandstand was part of a state-of-the-art racing complex also comprising a Clubhouse and Betting Ring that replaced the track's mid-century buildings and injected a sense of style into what previously had been an essentially sober and serviceable building type *(Figure 24)*.

The architect responsible for the complex was Herbert Langford Warren (1857-1917). Warren was a renowned figure in Boston's Arts and Crafts movement. His selection as architect for the Race Course was a telling choice. Warren was a respected architect. In fact, his appointment was the first of several progressive architecture and landscape practitioners that worked for the Association in the forthcoming decades. Warren had studied under one of the nineteenth century's most celebrated architects, H. H. Richardson, and by the time of his death in 1917 he was dean of Harvard's School of Architecture, where he had taught since 1893. By commissioning him to design its new buildings, the Saratoga Association identified itself as a sophisticated architectural patron. For the Saratoga Race Course, it seemed, no mere utilitarian shelter would do; it wanted to make a visual splash. Indeed, Warren transformed the face of the Race Course, creating a powerful architectural presence that has dominated the site since its 1892 opening day on July 25 *(Figure 25)*.

Almost certainly the motivation behind the comprehensive remodeling was a competitive one – to distinguish the Race Course from the multitude of nearby competitors. In 1892, *Outing* magazine wrote,

This country teems with racing associations of greater or lesser importance, from the Pacific to the Atlantic, from Maine to Texas. Scarcely a city of any size but has a race-course of some kind in close proximity to it, and many a settlement that hardly merits the name of village boasts its "track".[46]

Figure 28. South End Grounds, Boston, hosted professional baseball from 1871-1914. The "witch's cap" turrets of its distinctive double-decked grandstand (1888) may have served as a model for Saratoga's iconic roofline.

A host of tracks vied to draw New York's racegoers to its sidelines. Sheepshead Bay Race Track had been founded in Brooklyn in 1870; the Brighton Beach and Gravesend tracks in Coney Island had held races since 1879 and 1886 respectively; while the facilities of Jerome Park (1866-94) and Morris Park (1889-1904) in the Bronx were held to be particularly luxurious. The question remains, though, who was originally responsible for the commissioning of

Warren's complex? The idea of the brothel-owning, loose-living, old-time bookmaker Walbaum as an enlightened architectural patron does not somehow ring true. If he did commission other architectural works or move in au courant artistic circles, no evidence remains to suggest it. And, moreover, the building work was complete for the opening of the 1892 season, less than a year after he and his Hudson County Jockey Club associates assumed

control of the track. No supporting documentary evidence exists, but it does not seem unreasonable to hypothesize that Warren's designs stemmed from the brief leadership of Hearst and Arkell, and their well-publicized plans to invest in new buildings and stands, which came to fruition when the Saratoga Race Course acquired a stable leadership under Walbaum.

Of the Grandstand, Clubhouse and Betting Ring complex that Warren designed, only the Grandstand survives today. It is nestled, jewel-like in its proportions and ornate trusswork decoration, within the present Grandstand-Clubhouse complex. It is not only the oldest stand still in use in American thoroughbred racing, but the oldest continuously-used stand of any professional sport in the country.[47] While today the Grandstand-Clubhouse structure extends over a quarter of a mile along the track side, Warren's Grandstand was a mere 200 feet long.

The Grandstand was a wooden construction, roofed but open to all sides and the seating was raked to slope towards the track. The seating was accessed via five sets of double stairs running parallel to the front of the Grandstand and by wide staircases on its east and west ends. The basic structure was functional and spartan, little different to other grandstands of its age; but it was crowned with a strikingly unique feature – a vast slate roof supported by a timber trusswork system. The roof had a sweeping silhouette, dominated by a cluster of

"His improvement to the grounds were made lavishly and regardless of expense… [in] every direction new lawns, club house, betting ring and an entrance that rivals in horticultural beauty any race course in the world, sprung genii-like from the Walbaum touch."

Figure 29. Queen-Anne style house on Union Avenue, Saratoga.

sloping turrets at its center capped by golden finials in the shape of jockey shirts (since lost) *(Figures 26, 27)*. At each end of the Grandstand, the slate roof swept up into another pyramidical turret. This motif of steeply sloping peaks may have had several points of inspiration. Steep rooflines were a recurring feature of the buildings of Warren's mentor, H. H. Richardson,[48] but a more germane model may have been the grandstand of South End Grounds, Boston's baseball field built in 1888 *(Figure 28)*. Here, each

end of the roof was demarcated by a cluster of three "witch's cap" turrets.[49] The concept was very similar to that used by Warren at Saratoga, but the overall effect was less refined. At South End Grounds, the grouping of conical and pyramidical turrets was cluttered and awkward; at Saratoga, the roof subtlety rose into dynamic peaks, creating a rhythmical, fluid silhouette.

The prevalence of eccentric roof forms at this time was symptomatic of the widespread

popularity of the Queen Anne architectural style, of which steeply sloping roofs was a key feature. The Queen Anne dominated domestic architecture in the United States between circa 1880 and 1910. Originally derived from the work of nineteenth-century British architect, Norman Shaw, the style's loose and wide-ranging repertoire of characteristics included asymmetry, overhanging eaves, wrap-around porches, and circular, square or polygonal towers. By the 1880s, the Springs' own Union

Figure 31. The 1892 Clubhouse, seen from the infield.

Figure 30. The Victorian Grandstand's decorative timber frame with cross-bracing, chamfered posts and cast iron brackets.

Avenue was being populated by substantial Queen Anne houses, whose steeply-pitched roofs with projecting gables and gold-capped finials echoed the flavor of the grandstand Warren was to create at the racetrack *(Figure 29)*. Although modified by subsequent building campaigns, the visual power of Warren's Grandstand roofline continues to dominate the track to this day.

The roof was carried upon a heavy timber frame of exposed Howe trusses, with a timber king post at its peak. While the frame was undoubtedly a structural device, under Warren's skillful hand it was elevated to a decorative piece of design in its own right. Its most distinctive and unique feature was the cross-bracing that extended the front of the Grandstand along its roof plate *(Figure 30)*. Whilst undoubtedly a strengthening method, the criss-cross motif was also a singularly bold and effective device. Warren's inventive play with the timber truss system brought a winning charm to what was otherwise a plain interior.

On the upper landing of the rear of the building Walbaum constructed so-called "retiring rooms" for women and children – which notoriously functioned as a bookmaker's operation (women were not allowed in the main Betting Ring). Having a betting ring specifically for women and children was the stuff of scandal. "There have been some objectionable features to [the races]", the *New York Times* bemoaned in 1892,

notably that of the betting room for women. The spectacle of 75 women crowding into a small apartment to bet from 25 cents to $500 was not edifying, and has never in previous seasons been deemed necessary.[50]

Nellie Bly, the star reporter of the *New York World* took particular offense at the handicapped odds offered there compared to the gentlemen's Betting Ring. "When a horse won with odds something like 200 to 1", she protested, "there had been two bets sold in the women's pool-room, and the odds were only 40 to 1."

At the western end of the Grandstand, Warren designed a Clubhouse – the racetrack's most exclusive environment (replaced 1928) *(Figure 31)*. Its long slate roof with a peak at either end provided a continuation of the horizontality of the Grandstand's roof, but the relationship of the Clubhouse to the Grandstand was in other respects far more autonomous than the arrangement existing today. Built smaller, lower and

at angle to the Grandstand, the Clubhouse was a distinctly separate structure to the Grandstand. It was a two-story, timber-framed rectangular structure capped with a steep, slate gable roof pierced by three hip gable windows *(Figure 32)*. The two buildings were connected by a second-floor walkway, which led to the Clubhouse's festal veranda *(Figure 33)*. The elegant, curving, double-story veranda projected outwards on the trackside. An exposed timber frame upheld its roof, but the decorative trusswork of the Grandstand was not replicated here. Yet, as within the Grandstand, the system of posts, plates and diagonal braces evoked a pavilion of space. The unenclosed nature of these spaces not only capitalized on cooling breezes in the hot summer season, but also ensured an immediacy between the racegoers and the action of the track.

Like the Grandstand, the Clubhouse was also informed by the Queen Anne style. Its veranda was sheltered by overhanging eaves and at each end its roof rose into conical peaks topped by golden finials, two regular features of the eclectic style. The building's dark-colored walls clad with shingles likewise typified the Queen Anne. Other design influences were at work too. The long and low profile, overhanging eaves, and exposed timber

Figure 33. Clubhouse veranda, where Saratoga's elite racegoers dined overlooking the track.

structure of the complex equally revealed the contemporary vogue for Japonisme – the taste for the arts of Japan – within Warren's circle in the 1890s. Japan had opened its doors to the West in the 1850s, precipitating a flurry of American interest in its architecture. By the early 1880s, Boston was America's hub of the Japanese art movement. Enthusiastic local orientalists William Sturgis Bigelow, Ernest Fenellosa, and Edward S. Morse

established important collections which introduced the city to Japanese art and culture. Importantly, Morse's collection of photos and drawings of the country's buildings launched an interest in Japanese architecture. This enthusiasm was spearheaded by Warren's tutor, H. H. Richardson, arguably the first American architect to employ a sustained repertoire of Japanese inspiration. The Boston and Albany railroad stations, designed in the 1880s, were

Figure 34. The Betting Ring was part of Herbert Langford Warren's 1892 redevelopment. The monitor roof was added a decade later.

amongst Richardson's most thorough and successful explorations of the aesthetic, and it is known that Warren contributed to the design of at least one of these stations (Auburndale).[51] Warren's interest in Japonisme was even more pronounced in the third building he designed at Saratoga, the Betting Ring.

The betting pavilion stood at the opposite end of the Grandstand *(Figure 34)*. Demolished in 1963, it was an iconic structure in its own right. It was

an exposed timber-frame construction, with a rectangular paved groundplan roughly equal in length to the Clubhouse. It housed the stalls, or cages, of the bookmakers. Whilst not strictly within the law, the bookmakers were vital to the operation of the Race Course. All the betting at Saratoga (as at other major tracks) was handled by bookmakers, who, in exchange for a fee, were allowed to set up business at the course. Within the Betting Ring, each stall

was elevated upon stilts and bore the name of its bookmaker, below which hung the all-important blackboard itemizing the entries and odds of the day's races *(Figure 35)*. Clamoring to outbid one another, the bookmakers shouted to the crowd from their raised stalls creating what must have been an atmosphere not unlike a Moroccan souk.[52] The Betting Ring was open to all sides, but a long, low slate roof sheltered the bookmakers from above. Like the Clubhouse and Grandstand, the roof was the building's distinguishing motif. From a hipped peak, the slate roof sloped gently outwards into flaring, overhanging eaves supported by evenly-spaced posts with curved braces and exposed rafters. Its low, broad and swooping silhouette was the perfect complement to the horizontality and sloping planes of the Grandstand, and was a clear expression of the influence of Japanese design and of Richardson upon Warren's oeuvre at this time. Its similarity with Richardson's railroad stations is arresting. The series of stations – particularly South Framingham, Old Colony and Connecticut River Stations – visibly embodied the spirit of Japanese design in their low-hipped, slate-gabled roofs with deeply bracketed overhang and exposed wood trusses, and was a direct source for Saratoga's Betting

Figure 36. Field Stand, the furthest stand from the finishing post.

Figure 37. View from the Clubhouse towards the Judges' Stand.

Ring. A monitor roof with a narrow band of glazing was added a decade later to the pavilion to increase light levels within.

Further east of the Betting Ring, an additional stand was erected. The Field Stand, or "black stand" as it became known, was located on the stretch far from the finishing line and charged a lower entrance price than the main stand *(Figure 36)*. Existing at virtually every racetrack up and down the country, field stands were used by the African-American track community – jockeys, trainers, stable boys – and racegoers until the 1960s when the majority were razed under the impetus of the Civil Rights movement.[53] Lacking the architectural pretensions of the Grandstand, the Field Stand was a simple, functional structure of raked seating covered by a plain gable roof. Completing Walbaum's new track side complex was the judges' stand *(Figure 37)*. With a Queen Anne-style silhouette and choice of materials, it perfectly complemented the design of the other buildings. Erected between the track and the Grandstand half way along its length, the timber-framed tower was three-stories tall topped by a pitched pyramidical roof, that echoed the peaks of the Grandstand, upheld upon chamfered posts with carved cross bracing and rafters. At second-floor level, officials gathered upon a podium enclosed by double-cross wooden railings, from which stairs ascended to the small raised podium where the judges pontificated behind a wooden balustrade *(Figure 38)*.

The Race Course's stylish new buildings sat within a majestic new landscape setting, establishing the tradition of a well-tended, sylvan landscape that lives on today. Walbaum lavished attention on the landscape of the course, planting a deciduous hedge around the track and laying a lawn alongside it. Wooden-post fencing, graced with stately orbs, framed pathways which meandered through the expansive open lawn behind the Grandstand – the area known as the Back Yard - and encircled Warren's new Grandstand and the judges' stand. At the heart of the Back Yard was the Saddling Shed. Now known only through a handful of historic photographs which provide glimpses of the structure through maturing trees, it was a highly unusual pavilion.[54] The long, narrow structure was

GRAND STAND, SARATOGA RACE TRACK

217488

Figure 38. Judges' Stand

two stories tall, with a completely open ground floor covered by an upper level held aloft upon soaring, slender timber posts. The second story, to judge by the hazy photographs, was a shingle-clad, open loggia covered by a hipped slate roof which gave panoramic views across the Back Yard. It was accessed via the Grandstand by an elevated catwalk which extended from the top story of the Saddling Shed to the rear of the main stand. Encircling and camouflaging the shed was a thriving grove of deciduous trees. Planted in Morrissey's time, these trees created a landscape character of verdant shade that continues to distinguish the Back Yard to the present day.

Walbaum's tenure at Saratoga brought with it an architectural revolution. For the first time, the racetrack's pleasure-seeking patrons could enjoy the sport in surroundings not only commodious, but at the height of architectural fashion. "Since President Walbaum gave up his racing stable and started to improve the Saratoga Race Course his efforts have shown results that will live long after him," eulogized the Official Souvenir of the Saratoga Association in 1900,

His improvement to the grounds were made lavishly and regardless of expense... [in] every direction new lawns, club

house, betting ring and an entrance that rivals in horticultural beauty any race course in the world, sprung genii-like from the Walbaum touch.

This was Saratoga at its visual peak; an artistic golden age. Never before, nor indeed since, had the quality of its architectural and landscape design been matched.

The racetrack looked its best, but under the surface all was far from well. Walbaum's infamy caused a media storm, and a tidal wave of anti-gambling sentiment ensued. Many of the most prominent stables deserted Saratoga in disgust at Dutch Fred's administration, vowing not to return while he remained in charge. Racing programs languished, with great races disappearing altogether. The Spinaway, first run in 1881, was cancelled between 1892 and 1901. Likewise, the Alabama Stakes, which had appeared on the program since 1872, was abandoned between 1893 and 1901, except for a sole running in 1897. Even the Travers – the highlight of the summer meeting – flagged. Today the oldest stakes race for three year olds in the United States, the Travers had been run annually at Saratoga since 1864. Yet under Walbaum its value plummeted to a record low of $1,125 in 1895, and was not run at all in 1896,

1898, 1899 and 1900.[55] Saratoga's vacationists were themselves appalled that Walbaum postponed the opening race from 11.30am to 2.30pm to suit his own habit of late-night gambling. The social routine of the season was rocked.[56]

The Saratoga exposé by the *New York World*'s intrepid reporter, Nellie Bly, poured a tirade of invectives against the "Wild Vortex of Gambling and Betting by Men, Women and Children". In her article, "Our Wickedest Summer Resort", the country's most famous journalist lambasted Walbaum's horse racing paradise as a nexus of "touts, Criminals and Race-Track Riff-Raff Crazed by the Mania for Gold". A particular target of her invective was the women's pool room: "I believe in liberty and the right to do as one pleases, but I don't think I should like to see such an assemblage again, even at the day of judgment".[57]

The 1890s was an architectural golden era for the Race Course, yet by the end of the century Saratoga's splendor was wilting. The track drew an unprofitable and insalubrious crowd and the resort as a whole was tarnished. But, this condition was not to last long. The Spa was about to secure its own knight in shining armor, and a new halcyon age was soon to dawn.

SARATOGA RACING ASSOCIATION.

WATER JUMP IN FRONT OF GRAND STAND.

RACING DURING JULY AND AUGUST IN EACH YEAR.

Figure 39. "Gilded Age" poster.

CHAPTER FIVE
SARATOGA'S GILDED AGE

Saratoga's savior came in the form of politician, speculator and scion of one of the country's most prominent families – William Collins Whitney (1841-1904). Whitney was the public-spirited lodestar of New York society. A graduate of Yale and Harvard Law School, he racked up a distinguished record for exposing fraud as the corporate counsel of New York City; served as secretary of the Navy under President Cleveland; and was held as a suitable candidate for Democratic presidential nomination. He made his fortune in the heady days of industrial expansion, holding major positions in the American Tobacco Company, Mergenthaler Linotype, Metropolitan Steamship, Morton Trust, U. S. Guaranty Trust, and the New York City transit system. Together with partners Thomas Fortune Ryan and P. A. B. Widener, by the mid-1900s essentially all the street railways of Manhattan and the Bronx were under Whitney's sway. He came to thoroughbred racing late in life, but when he turned his attention to the sport of kings in 1893 he did so with gusto. His ascendency was nothing short of phenomenal. Hiring the best trainers and buying the best horses, by 1901 he ranked amongst America's most successful owners,

62

Figure 40. Clubhouse, Grandstand, Betting Ring and Field Stand, seen from the air, following improvement works by new Saratoga Association president, William C. Whitney.

Figure 41. "General Plan of the Saratoga Race Course Property", Charles Leavitt, 1902. Leavitt realigned the circuit by 25° and planned a new training track at Horse Haven, later dubbed Oklahoma.

and momentous transformation of the track *(Figure 40)*. The buildings, backstretch and landscape were coordinated in an integrated design under the direction of landscape engineer Charles Leavitt (1871-1928). Described as "a rare combination of engineer, artist and diplomat", Leavitt was a dynamic choice to drive Saratoga's renaissance.[59] His multifarious career began with railroad engineering, sewer construction and infrastructure planning before, in 1897, embarking upon an enormously successful career as a landscape designer, receiving a host of public and private commissions. In fact, Leavitt could turn his hand to designing just about anything. He designed parks in Philadelphia and Colorado Springs; campuses for the Universities of Georgia and South Carolina; city plans for Garden City and Long Beach in New York; the Forbes Field Stadium in Pittsburgh; and country estates for Charles M. Schwab in Pennsylvania and for Foxhall Keene in New York.[60] He was one of the founding professors of Columbia University's inaugural landscape architecture program and, within his municipal planning work, became one of the leading practitioners of the City Beautiful

even winning the English Derby. "It is exceedingly doubtful," wrote journalist W. H. Rowe in 1901, "if our turf has ever experienced the acquisition of a gentleman of more unique prominence or of more thoroughly desirable individuality."[58]

In 1900 Whitney joined forces with New York financier and Saratoga partisan, Richard T. Wilson Jr., to rescue Saratoga Race Course, and the following

year the vilified Walbaum sold out for a reported $365,000 to a new collective headed by Whitney. The Whitney name brought a new sense of respectability to the faded track that allayed many of the anti-gambling lobbyists. Indeed, everything about the Springs suddenly became gilt-edged.

No sooner than the deal was done, the reborn Saratoga Association embarked upon an immediate

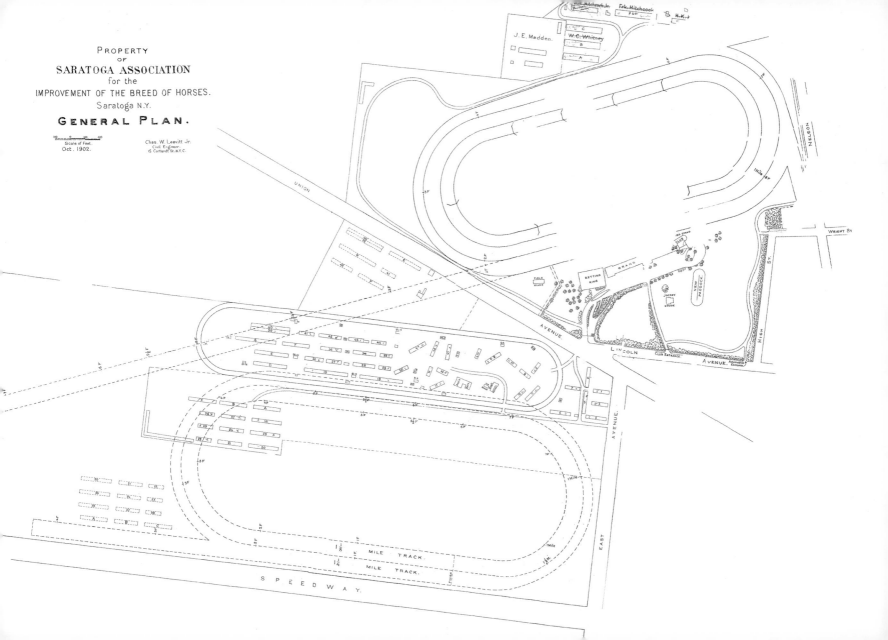

PROPERTY
OF
SARATOGA ASSOCIATION
for the
IMPROVEMENT OF THE BREED OF HORSES.
Saratoga N.Y.
GENERAL PLAN.

Scale of Feet.
Oct. 1902.

Chas. W. Leavitt, Jr.
Civil Engineer.
15 Cortlandt St. N.Y.C.

Figure 42. Clubhouse, Grandstand and Betting Ring following William C. Whitney's expansion.

Figure 43. Grandstand detail

Westchester County as his model, he created a track "thoroughly scientific and up to date". "The chief alteration in the Saratoga track, in the minds of horse owners and trainers is the enlargement of the track itself from a mile course to one of a mile, and a furlong," wrote the *New York Daily Tribune* (August 3, 1902). The whole track was rotated 25 degrees and slid westwards, and a turf steeplechase course was inserted into the infield.[61] The Grandstand and Clubhouse too were made bigger and better. According to the *New York Daily Tribune*,

The old stand was so situated that toward the end of the afternoon the rays of the setting sun shone full into the eyes of the spectators, and made the last races of the day difficult to see. In order to right this wrong, the stand was cut into three pieces and moved bodily to a site nearer the track facing almost directly south. Two large additions were then built between these sections, so that the stand has been lengthened by 160 additional feet to a total length of 750 feet, with a width of fifty feet.[62]

New seating was inserted into the additional sections, increasing by fifty per cent the Grandstand's capacity to 6,000 *(Figure 42)*. The five staircases that led from the tiered seating to the track apron were replaced with seven new ones, which sported large arched windows to light the administrative spaces beneath the stairs *(Figure 43)*. The remodeled ground floor was lighter and more

Movement. With a steady stream of clients that included the likes of Walter P. Chrysler and John D. Rockefeller, Leavitt was a sought-after professional amongst East Coast society. Like Herbert Langford Warren a decade earlier, Leavitt was a well-known, well-respected name in his field and in hiring him, Whitney and the Saratoga Association showed their determination that the racetrack would once again be aligned with all that was fashionable amongst the reigning social elite. Moreover, Leavitt was building an impressive record as a racetrack designer. He designed courses at Sheepshead Bay, Belmont, Toronto, and Empire City, plus, in 1901, Whitney's private track in Long Island.

Leavitt produced the earliest-known master plan of Saratoga Race Course *(Figure 41)*. He first turned his attention to the main circuit itself. With the same principles used at the Empire Track in

Figure 44. Judges' Stand. A shorter, stockier stand replaced the 1892 version to improve sightlines from the Grandstand.

The club members of the association are to enjoy what might truly be called a new clubhouse which, like the new grand stand, has been rebuilt so that spectators seated on its verandas may enjoy a clear view of the track without being blinded by the afternoon sun. The rooms of the clubhouse contain all that is needed for the convenience or refreshment of the members.[64]

A handsome ladies' parlor and a buffet area stood either side of its main staircase.

The enlargement works were no mean feat. "[It] involved the purchase of all of our side of High Street," one resident later reminisced. "Our house was placed on rollers and, in a confusion of shouting workmen and straining horses, swung majestically up the street and over a block to a new site."[65] Yet what is striking in terms of the improvement works is how little of Warren's 1892 complex was changed. Whilst the Grandstand was enlarged, the sweeping planes of its distinctive roof were left undisturbed and the structure was merely refreshed with a coat of dark red stain and bottle-green paint. The changes applied to the Clubhouse similarly impacted very little upon its external appearance. Given the huge funds Whitney and the Saratoga Association were prepared to pour into upgrading the facility, it is evident that they respected the 1892 scheme, both in terms of its functionality and its beauty.

To the rear of the Clubhouse a vast new Saddling Shed, 240 feet by 72 feet, replaced the earlier version *(Figure 45)*. Containing 25 stalls, it was here that the horses were saddled and paraded on rainy days until 1963. It was a simple, timber-framed structure, open

spacious, and included a new café, dining room and kitchen, telegraph room and secretary's office.[63]

The judging stand before the Grandstand was also replaced at this time or shortly after. It was a simple, two-story, square structure that shared the slate roof, timber frame and shingle walls that typified the track's architecture *(Figure 44)*. At the lower register, a veranda encircled the small building. From the upper story a viewing deck overlooked the track, shielded from the sun by a canopy. Since it was a much shorter and stockier stand than its tall Victorian predecessor, it improved sightlines for racegoers in the Grandstand behind.

The spectator experience was furthermore improved by a remodeling of the Clubhouse, which shifted its roof upwards by five feet:

to the sides bar a low wooden picket fence. Wooden posts supported an exposed, heavy timber Howe truss system, akin to the spirit of the Grandstand and Clubhouse, which upheld a slate mansard roof. Its dark interior, scent-laden with the smell of straw, was illuminated by a row of louvered small triangular dormer windows which pierced the roof.

The Saddling Shed stood at the heart of the Paddock, a vast lawn behind the Clubhouse within the wider expanse of the Back Yard. The Paddock was the site of the great Saratoga tradition that took place from the earliest days of the Saratoga Association - the saddling of the horses under the trees surrounded by the racetrack community of jockeys, grooms, trainers, owners, and clientele.[66] The groupings of tall trees that populated the Paddock served as informal stalls and exercise rings where the pre-race saddling ritual took place, unless of course rain drove it under the cover of the Saddling Shed. Anyone and everyone could here get within touching distance of the equine stars; no fences separated the public. "On days when popular favorites are running," recorded *Everybody's Magazine* in 1904, "the benches under the pines, the spaces under the walking sheds, are occupied by the lady of Saratoga and her friends." In the latter half of the twentieth century this area became increasingly

Figure 46. The informal, unrestricted comingling of horses, grooms, jockeys and fans in the Paddock beside the Saddling Shed.

Figure 47. and Figure 48. The pre-race saddling ritual under the Back Yard's dense tree covering. The Back Yard was a vast open lawn undelineated by fencing or hardscaped pathways.

infiltrated by a jumble of booths, stands and wooden fencing, but until this time it was an open grassy tract dominated only by trees. Photographs from the 1940s and 1950s document the great pre-race communion under the shade of the Paddock's green canopy *(Figures 46, 47, 48)*. Chain link fencing was introduced in the 1950s to delineate the horse paths to the Clubhouse but the Paddock was as yet still unobstructed by fencing.

Leavitt was careful to keep all formal pathways and roadways out of the Paddock. He did, though, establish a network of circulation routes and entrances around the perimeter of the Back Yard. Under Leavitt's plan, the Back Yard was entered via one of three entrances: the original main gate on Union Avenue opposite the Horse Haven entrance; a new "club" entrance leading from Lincoln Avenue more directly to the Grandstand and Clubhouse; and

a new "automobile" entrance, at the far corner of Lincoln Avenue and High Street. The latter entrance was indicative of the new invention of the motor car, whose presence was increasingly catered for in the environs of the Frontside by the installation of hard paving. At the main entrance, a new gate created an impressive, well-groomed street frontage *(Figure 49)*. From the moment the Race Course came in sight, Leavitt and the Saratoga Association were intent that visitors would be dazzled by the refinement of its physical setting. The iron gate hung from two red brick piers capped with round stone finials, making for an unpretentious yet robust and venerable entrance to the track. Inside the gateway was a cast-iron fountain featuring three stacked bowls adorned with seahorses on a seven-foot circular base, which had stood there since 1880. The wooden fence that had delineated the Saratoga Association's property was torn down, and replaced with an iron picket-style fence, eight-and-a-half feet tall. A new ticket stand was built at the main entrance, replacing the old ticket office which had stood outside the entry *(Figure 50)*. The new office was a two-tiered, polygonal Victorian pavilion. The lower register was comprised of a central drum housing the ticket office. A gently sloping hip roof with overhanging eaves skirted the drum, supported at each corner by slender posts. The pavilion was topped by a tall lantern cupola, formed of a band of glazed windows and a turreted roof capped with a finial. The jockey's cottage, close to the Saddling Shed, was also remodeled.

Substantial sums were spent to create a garden idyll in the track environs. The degree to which the Saratoga Association prided itself on creating

Figure 49. Union Avenue entrance, early 1900s.

a bucolic setting cannot be overestimated. "Great care has been taken," commended the *Daily Gazette* in August 1902, "to retain the handsome wooded appearance, and more trees and luxuriant foliage lend additional beauty to the entrance of the park."[67] Even at this relatively early stage in the course's lifetime, its sylvan setting was valued as a key ingredient of its charm and persona. Whitney and Leavitt did not lavish attention solely upon the track itself; rather the overall visitor experience was

meticulously considered. The lawns and flower beds were refreshed with fresh sods and plantings; and trees and shrubs were planted to define the Back Yard's walkways and roadways and create welcome shade near the Saddling Shed. Journalist Frank W. Thorp noted that "on every side the gardener has helped beautify the natural charms of a lovely park, and the eye is delighted and soothed".[68] In 1902 the much-cherished features of the infield lake and landscape were created.[69]

The Daily Gazette might have been employing poetic license when it eulogized that "at first visitors will scarcely recognize the place", when the new season opened on August 4, 1902. The fundamental architectural character of its Victorian buildings remained; but a new lease of life had indeed been infused into the Race Course. And contemporaries welcomed these changes with open arms. The Saratoga Association, one *New York Times* correspondent marveled, improved "the grounds and entrances to such an extent that it would be difficult to make them better or more inviting" (June 1, 1902). Local, regional and national newspapers showered praise upon the redevelopment. According to the *New York Daily Tribune*, "the renovated and enlarged

Figure 51. Residence Cottage, Sanford Court, built 1901.

"It was well worth $3 to any one who could spare it merely to see the beautiful grounds, the smart contingent, the notables of society, the turf and business, and the little army of betting men and bookmakers."

Saratoga course has come to be called the New Saratoga, and the name is most appropriate."[70]

The transformation was, moreover, extended beyond the environs of the Frontside and Back Yard; the 1901 takeover had prominent repercussions on the physical environment of Saratoga's backstretch as well. With "Dutch Fred" Walbaum at the helm, 20 acres were added to the backstretch property and several barns were built. But it was after Whitney's takeover in 1901 that the land attracted substantial investment. Several new building styles were introduced, but the most decisive changes issued from the revised approach to planning. Under the new leadership, the Race Course property nearly doubled in size, most visibly with the expansion of stabling beyond the immediate confines of the original trotting track to land south of Union Avenue. The new land was developed following the guidelines set by Leavitt's master plan. A clear disparity in land organization between the nineteenth-century construction and the new master plan was that of the creation of private stabling compounds set around courtyards, beginning with Sanford Court in 1901.

After establishing a fortune as a carpet magnate, Stephen Sanford and his son John had been breeding and racing thoroughbreds since the early 1880s with

Figure 52. One of two identical barns, Sanford Court, built 1901.

kitchen, clad with clapboards on the exterior and tongue-and-groove boards internally *(Figure 51)*. Like Walbaum's Grandstand and Clubhouse built in the preceding decade, its references to the eclectic Queen Anne aesthetic were numerous. In particular, it has a steeply pitched roof covered with slate and gable ends pierced with a single diamond-shaped window. A veranda with a broad, overhanging slate roof supported by lathe-turned columns with carved brackets, wrapped around the two-story house and connected it with the kitchen annex. The two identical barns equally reflected the Queen Anne vogue for exaggerated height, steeply-gabled slate roofs and capricious windows. Architecturally, they are markedly different from those nineteenth-century barns north of Union Avenue and they exhibit the second barn typology existing at the Race Course. Each Sanford barn featured 20 single-loaded stalls entirely surrounded by a wrap-around shed row that functioned as a sheltered walking ring and mimicked the wrap-around porches of domestic Queen Anne buildings *(Figure 52)*. Distinctively, they had a double-level roof composed of a gable over the stalls and a less-steeply inclined hipped slate roof over the shed row, with the two divided by a strip of clerestory windows. Each gable end was pierced by a diamond-shaped vent, promoting air circulation in the higher regions of the stables. The nineteenth-century stables at Horse Haven lacked these fanciful details. They had no clerestory windows and only a

remarkable success. The purple and gold stripes of the Sanford silks were a regular fixture at Saratoga's races. Sanford Court, built to house the family's thoroughbreds during the summer season, was built on a two-and-a-half acre private lot on the west side of Nelson Avenue. It was a small, self-contained complex, perfectly suited to the Sanfords' needs, consisting of two large barns and small residence that formed three sides of a rectangular courtyard.

It is unique amongst the private stable complexes that subsequently took root at Saratoga. Not only did it continue to be privately operated until the 1940s when others had been conveyanced to the Saratoga Association, but moreover its architectural style was unparalleled within the backstretch community. Its sophisticated design embraced the spirit of the popular Queen Anne style. The residence was a tall two-story house with adjacent single-story

Figure 53. Horses relax amongst Clare Court's vertiginous evergreens, c1940.

single shed row which ran along the front length, covered by the overhang of the gable roof.

Sanford Court was not the sole private complex to be built in these years. "Many of the wealthy New York Turfites now are building private stables in or close by the track," noted the *New York Times*,

[It] is an innovation here, but a popular one, and one that promises to grow in favor, as for horsemen who can afford to build barns of their own many of the dangers and annoyances of training while occupying public structures are avoided.[71]

The most expensive of the stables was doubtlessly that built by August Belmont Jr. circa 1902, located on the backstretch across from the Grandstand. The Belmonts were a racing dynasty in turn-of-the-century New York, as testified by the naming of Belmont Park and the Belmont Stakes in honor of August Sr. His son inherited not only his father's vast banking fortune but moreover his avid interest in the turf and his legacy to the sport was superlative. A brilliant scholar of bloodlines, August Jr. ranked amongst the world's best breeders; champions of the likes of Man O'War, Tracery and Hourless passed through his stables. He was chairman of the Jockey Club for 30 years, founder of

Sheepshead Bay and Belmont Park tracks, and head of New York's first Racing Commission.

The Belmonts had in fact owned a stable at Saratoga since the late 1870s at the southwest corner of the original track. However, when the improvement plans drawn up by Whitney's engineer, Charles Leavitt, necessitated the relocation of the main track onto this land, a land exchange was negotiated between the Saratoga Association and the Belmonts.[72] On his new, 13-acre parcel of land, August Jr. built a comprehensively-designed facility, sequestered from the outside world. Originally nicknamed "Surcingle" in regard to the leather strap used to accustom young horses to girth pressure, the stables are now known as Clare Court in honor of Tom and Anne Clare who served as successive superintendents of the track from 1924 to 1960. Although its gardens and tennis court no longer exist, the barns and residence that made up Belmont's self-contained facility stand to this day. Akin to the arrangement at the Sanford stable, three barns and a house were structured around a courtyard *(Figure 53)*. A blacksmith's workshop and additional small dwelling completed the ensemble.[73] The whole was encircled by a broad

half-mile long track – Saratoga's second training track. Given the track's seasonal nature, this was an elaborate facility indeed.

Access to the court was gained by the complex's most unusual and innovative feature – a tunnel which led from the backstretch entrance drive to surface in the center of the Surcingle courtyard *(Figure 54)*. Whilst several roadways now cross the land, this was originally the sole means of entry and exit and an ingenious device to ensure that horses exercising on the track were not disrupted by the passage of traffic. The careful consideration given to ensure the smooth running of the stables is in evidence in every design feature of the court. The track was screened from the outside, providing for the least possible disturbance for the animals and for utmost privacy from the potentially prying eyes of rival stables. The sole vantage point from which the entire practice track could be surveyed was the cupola upon the Belmont's cottage at the center of the courtyard. This late-Victorian feature, though, sadly no longer exists.[74]

Since it ceased to be used by the Belmonts, the cottage has been appropriated first by the track's veterinarians and later as a female dormitory.

Despite internal modifications that have resulted from these shifts in use, the exterior of the house remains largely as it would have looked a century ago. Two-stories tall, the cottage had the steeply pitched hipped roofs and overhanging eaves common to the other Race Course properties of the era.

On the opposite side of the courtyard stood a single barn constructed solely for the stabling of driving horses and carriages – Saratoga's third stable type. While now used to house thoroughbreds, its first purpose is indicated by the large, double carriage doors on its front elevation surmounted by a curving or "eyebrow" roofline. Its slate roof was pierced with gabled dormers and triangular louvered vents, and its walls were clad in clapboard. Flanking the carriage stable, the remaining two barns were identical. The long, 24-stall single-loaded barns were topped by a slate-covered gable roof over a double-height space *(Figure 55)*. Below, projected a separate, hipped-gable roof covering a wrap-around shed row which acted as a sheltered walking ring. The rounded building corners and chamfered posts betokened the measures taken to prevent the injury of horses walking around the circuit. Vertical tongue-and-groove clad the walls.[75] This is the

Figure 54. A tunnel provided subterranean access to Clare Court.

fourth stable formula detectable at Saratoga, and one that was also utilized for the barns of Madden Court, a contemporary stabling block built by celebrated horseman John E. Madden.[76]

The likes of Belmont, Sanford and Madden were no ordinary turfmen; they were the most prominent, most influential and wealthiest horsemen of the day. Thus their construction of private stables at the track is telling proof of the widespread confidence innately awakened by the Whitney name that the dark days

of the Walbaum tenure were dead and buried and a new gilded age was beginning. "The private training quarters represent a great outlay that never would have been made," the *New York Times* confirmed, "had not the owners been convinced that racing will continue here on even a grander and better scale than that on which the sport had been conducted for thirty-eight years."[77]

Whitney himself considered the improvement of the backstretch a fundamental facet of his grand plan for Saratoga. With a surplus of $80-100,000 by the close of the 1902 season, the new leadership turned its attention to the land north of Union Avenue – to Horse Haven and beyond. In October that year Whitney purchased a substantial tract of land stretching east of East Avenue to the Crosby Property and from Union Avenue at the south to the Speedway (Fifth Avenue) in the north. Added to the existing Horse Haven property, this amounted to 120 acres. Inspired by the sales held at Kentucky, Tennessee and Californian breeding centers, the Association visualized Saratoga playing host to a great national sale. With Leavitt's help, Whitney aimed to transform Saratoga into the nation's leading thoroughbred training and sales center.[78]

Figure 56. The Oklahoma track, designed 1902, expanded Horse Haven's training facilities.

"It is a tradition among horsemen that horses that have had the advantage of the Saratoga climate for a month or so in the summer, are usually in better condition to contest for the autumn events upon the tracks near New York City," wrote the *Saratogian* in 1902.[79] Yet the 1847 Horse Haven track was woefully inadequate for modern training. With whiplash bends, horses could not pick up speed with any safety. The 1902 land purchase offered the opportunity to construct the Race Course's third exercising track plus additional stables, modernizing Saratoga into a grand training facility. Distanced far from the Frontside, the new grounds and track became known as Oklahoma *(Figure 56)*. It was, after all, an era when "Oklahoma seemed as remote as Mars".[80] The track was an immediate success. "Horse Haven had been so transformed that the oldest racing man wouldn't know it," rhapsodized the *Schenectady Gazette*.[81] Adjoining the Oklahoma track, the Saratoga Association built the Race Course's biggest individual stabling group designed to be let to breeding and auction companies during the sales. The stables repeated on a larger scale the basic formula of the earliest Horse Haven barns, but the group clearly demonstrates the shift in organization by the early twentieth century towards long, linear rows of stabling. Today, Oklahoma is made up of 21 barns, 23 bunkhouses and several support structures interspersed with shade and hedgerow plantings.

Saratoga was already renowned as a wooded retreat, but enhancing the pastoral side of its character played a key role in Whitney's vision for the backstretch. A grassy boulevard lined with a parade of evenly-spaced trees was created between the Horse Haven track and Oklahoma. According to the *Saratogian,* 2,500 trees were planted on the newly-acquired land.[82] The November 1902 edition of *Munsey's Magazine* effervesced that "beautiful Horse Haven, noted the country over for its pure air and the enormous benefit which accrues to the thoroughbreds summoned there, was made an Eden." Indeed, Saratoga's continued reputation as a sylvan setting has much to do with the extensive planting that went on in these golden years of transformation *(Figure 57)*. For instance, Madden Court, the private stabling facility built circa 1902, exemplifies the wooded charm that has come to characterize the barns. Mature rows of deciduous

Figure 57. The tree-shaded ambience of the backstretch.

trees along the roadsides and between the barns provide a canopy of dappled shade. The species are diverse, including lindens, sugar maples, silver maples, honey locusts and elm. Likewise, the well-preserved grove of pines, spruces and cedars in Campfire Court is indispensible to its historic atmosphere. Spanning the complete history of the racetrack, the large overhanging trees grow in clusters throughout the court, creating naturally shaded walking rings. In recent decades, trees have suffered from age, disease and a growing vehicular presence on the property, yet the atmosphere that prevails remains one of a secluded, green idyll. Narrow, even rows of vertiginous oaks, maples and spruces create vistas across the site and foster an intimate scale which has rendered the place so cherished by generation after generation.

"The track was always a beautiful sport," wrote the November 1902 edition of *Munsey's Magazine*, "under the magic touch of its new owners it became a paradise." The building and landscaping works both in the public and training areas testified to substantial investment on behalf of the new owners which gave a clear message of their ambitions for the track.[83] Pushing its recent past aside, Saratoga Race Course was entering a new century and looking towards a new future.

Figure 58. Racegoers watched the pre-race ritual as horses processed along the Back Yard's meandering pathways.

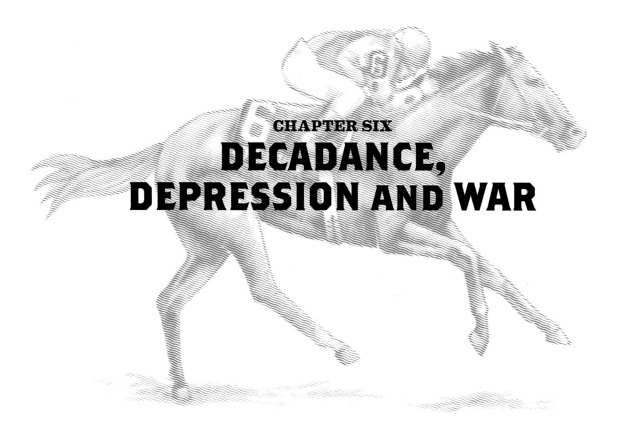

CHAPTER SIX
DECADANCE, DEPRESSION AND WAR

By the end of the twentieth century's first decade, the golden touch of William C. Whitney and Charles Leavitt had pitched Saratoga Race Course to new heights of acclaim. But this idyll was soon disturbed, for a reformist storm was brewing country-wide within the thoroughbred industry. On March 21, 1911, representatives of the Coney Island Jockey Club (Sheepshead Bay Race Track),

Westchester Racing Association (Belmont Park), Queens County Jockey Club (Aqueduct Racetrack), Empire City Racing Association (Empire City Race Track), Metropolitan Jockey Club (Jamaica Race Track) and the Saratoga Association made an announcement - there would be no thoroughbred racing that year because of the so-called Directors Liability Law. Three years earlier, the State had passed an anti-gambling bill against the soliciting or recording of bets in a fixed place and quoting betting odds openly. However, the Agnew-Hart Act, as the bill was named, did not satisfy the zeal of the right-wing legislators and moral lobbyists for it could be interpreted in such a way to allow oral betting. Thus in 1910 the passing of an amended act restricted all forms of wagering and mandated that racetrack directors would face criminal charges if anyone were caught gambling on their grounds. Thoroughbred racing in New York crumbled. Without betting, the crowds vanished. The tracks could not survive without the bookmakers' fees and the entrance receipts, and for the next two years no race meetings were held in the state.

The ramifications for the sport were substantial. By this time, Maryland and Kentucky were the sole states to allow horse race wagering. Many of the best owners, trainers, and jockeys were driven to Europe. No less grave were the economic ramifications. Saratoga Springs was particularly affected. Without its racing season, several businesses were bankrupted, hotels were left with empty rooms, and real estate values sunk. Much to the chagrin of the anti-gambling faction, though, in 1913 a loophole

was opened. A state court ruled that the law forbade only written bets, opening the way for oral betting, and thus allowing the return of thoroughbred racing to New York. When Saratoga reopened in 1913, the bookmakers and their helpers returned to the town by special train to be greeted by a brass-band welcome from the relieved community.

By the close of World War I, horse racing in the US was embarking upon a great revival. In the 1920s, the number of thoroughbreds doubled, the total races increased and purses rocketed. It was moreover the great age of the sports' heroes – Sir Barton, Man O'War, Exterminator, and Mad Play amongst others. Once again, New York was the trailblazer state. It had the most racetracks, drew the largest crowds and the biggest handle. In fact, the term "Big Apple" was derived from thoroughbred racing in the 1920s.[84] The Saratoga Association President, Richard T. Wilson, was praised for encouraging the return of so many big stables to the Spa after its dark days.[85] Some tracks, however, never recovered from the crisis. Notably, the once thriving Brighton Beach, Gravesend and Sheepshead Bay tracks did not reopen.

Whitney never had to endure the dark days of Saratoga. He died in 1904 from appendicitis

at the age of 62. His leadership of the Saratoga Association had effected a lasting framework for the architecture and landscape of the track, and very few changes were made to it until the 1920s and 1930s. These decades ushered in a flurry of activity in which the Race Course underwent a phase of continuous expansion and improvement that lasted over 20 years. This area of activity began in 1919 with the purchase of a parcel of land between Union and Lincoln Avenues at the western boundary of the Saratoga Association property. By now Saratoga's millionaires drove Stutz Bearcats instead of four-in-hands and the land, known as the Sheehan-Wells property after its previous owners, was destined to become the "auto parking area". To spearhead its transformation, the Association engaged civil engineer S. J. Mott (1869-1942). Mott was a local man, having gained experience building the Saranac and Lake Placid Railroad (1892) and overseeing the building of the Saratoga Springs sewage disposal plant.[86] His 1919 plan for the Sheehan-Wells site survives today. The road which bisected the lot – Lincoln Avenue – was removed and a large parking lot was created, bounded by a six-feet high picket fence with brick posts which echoed the fencing

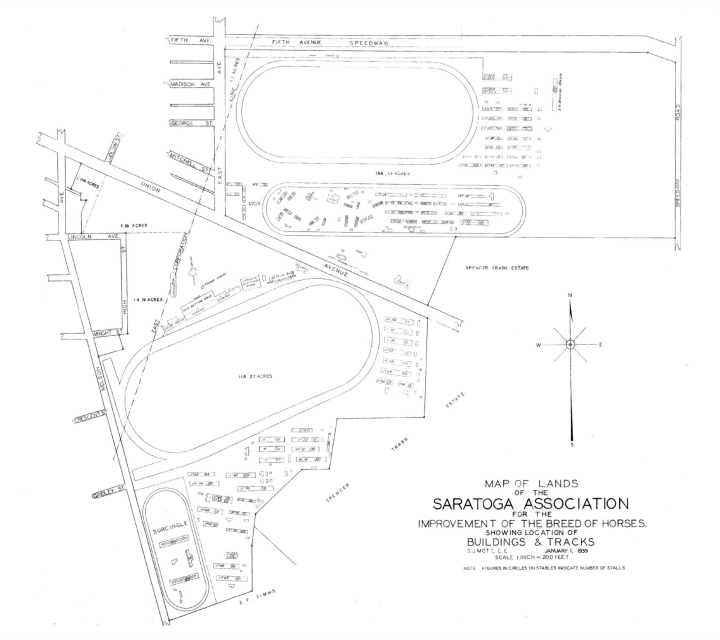

MAP OF LANDS
OF THE
SARATOGA ASSOCIATION
FOR THE
IMPROVEMENT OF THE BREED OF HORSES.
SHOWING LOCATION OF
BUILDINGS & TRACKS
S. J. MOTT, C.E.   JANUARY 1, 1939
SCALE 1 INCH = 200 FEET.

NOTE   FIGURES IN CIRCLES ON STABLES INDICATE NUMBER OF STALLS

Figure 60. Frontside buildings, including 1928 Clubhouse designed by Samuel Adams Clark.

he was responsible for the earliest extant drawings for the infield planting. Semi-circular hedges skirted the outer edge of the infield, delineating the steeplechase course; a small pond was shown; and sprinklers were carefully spaced along the circuit. He produced several site plans of the Race Course property, which today yield invaluable panoramas of the track's evolution in these years *(Figure 59).*[89]

Mott's last plan for the site dates to January 1939, several months too early to detail an important accretion to the Saratoga Association's property made in June of that year. The Oklahoma Annex, as this accretion became known, was a 5.9-acre lot located just north of the Oklahoma track which had been owned by the Fasig-Tipton Company, America's oldest thoroughbred auctioneers. In August 1917, Fasig-Tipton had begun conducting annual yearling sales at the Springs. Ever since, this has been ranked amongst the world's foremost horse auctions, with youngsters such as Man O'War, Raise a Native, Natalma, Miswaki and Black Tie Affair having passed through its sales ring. When the Company purchased the parcel now known as the Oklahoma Annex in 1926, it constructed two stables and a bunkhouse which still survive to this day. Modeled upon the same design as Fasig-Tipton's other stables across East Avenue, these two barns made for a discernable departure from the Race Course's other examples and form the eighth barn typology

style introduced under Whitney's improvements at the beginning of the century. Mott's plan provided for two Union Avenue gateways into the auto area, the most westerly of which opened onto a newly-created entrance drive leading to the Clubhouse which Mott planted with long rows of evenly-spaced poplars. An important facet of Mott's concept for the site was the planting of an extensive tree canopy and covering of shrubbery,

approximating the ambience of the Back Yard and softening the provisions made for the burgeoning ownership of cars in this period.[87] As the century progressed, increasingly arrangements were made for the use of cars at Saratoga. By the 1940s, as many as eight driveways punctuated the Union Avenue perimeter.[88]

Mott continued to work for the Saratoga Association for the next 20 years. In 1929, for instance,

Figure 61. "Plan of Clubhouse and Grandstand", S. J. Mott, 1936.

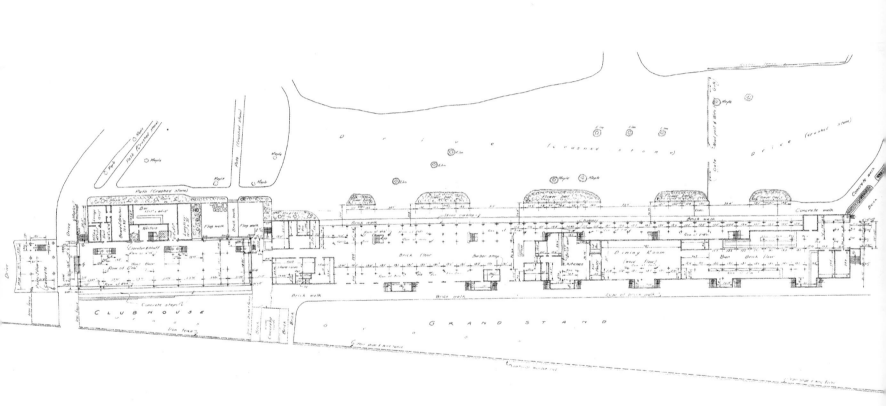

Figure 62. The 1928 Clubhouse as seen today.

of the site. They were double-loaded, rather than single-rowed, and had no windows; ventilation came instead from louvered vents at each gable end.

The most pronounced changes to the Saratoga Association property were not, though, those of the backstretch but rather those confined to the public arenas. From the late 1920s, the Frontside as Dutch Fred or Whitney would have known it changed considerably. It was a time of growing attendances at the Race Course, and the demand for boxes outstripped supply. "Society Throngs Clubhouse at Spa; Stands Prove Inadequate for Crowds", ran a *New York Times* headline on August 21, 1927. The 1892 Queen Anne Clubhouse, while picturesque, was simply too small and plans for modernization were soon afoot. In 1927 the architect Samuel Adams Clark, of the firm LaFarge, Warren and Clark, was employed to design a substantially larger replacement, and Walbaum's Clubhouse was demolished to make way for it. Measuring 211 feet in length by 44 feet in width, the large building increased Clubhouse facilities considerably; it now housed 1,200 box seats with a total capacity of 3,000 *(Figures 60, 61)*. It was the epitome in modern comfort and technology, using steel construction and including the extravagant feature of an electric elevator. The steel frame was clad in dark timber

Figure 63. The 1928 Clubhouse was much larger than its Victorian predecessor.

and shingles, which mimicked the deep coloring of the Grandstand. Yet despite brimming with all the mod-cons of the age, the building arguably lacked the aesthetic finesse of its predecessor. The new Clubhouse made few architectural concessions to harmonize with the distinctive profile of the Victorian Grandstand. At three stories tall, it towered over the Grandstand. Gone was the curving outline of the old Clubhouse; this was a

long, rectangular structure from which projected a kitchen annex, smaller and lower in profile, at the rear. The Clubhouse was roofed by a simple slate mansard roof with overhanging eaves, whose silhouette was broken only by a single finial at each end of the ridge *(Figure 62)*. It had none of the drama or imagination of the sloping planes of the Victorian structures. Neither was the decorative trusswork of the Grandstand replicated. Arguably, the new

Figure 64. Horse Path, Clubhouse. Horses traversed through the Clubhouse en route from the Paddock to the track. Today this forms part of the ground-floor terrace.

structure marked the end of Saratoga's architectural golden age.

One of the principal points of departure from the original Clubhouse was that Clark's design was no longer disjointed from the Grandstand structure. It abutted the latter to form one continuous length running parallel to the track and the connection between the two buildings was far more fluid than had previously been the case. Direct passage between the two structures was made possible via an octagonal tower, which served as the new judges' tower. Necessitating the removal of the Grandstand's western turret, the tower was integrated within the eastern end of the Clubhouse and projected upwards through its roof *(Figure 63)*. Capped with a slate pavilion roof, it gave a commanding view over the track. The judges' stand rendered redundant, it was taken down. The most distinctive aspect of the building's design was its western end. Saratoga's race-going elite entered by an august-looking porch at its west side, referred to as the "Landing Stage". The "Landing Stage" brought a touch of ancient Greece to Saratoga's clubhouse. It consisted of two rows of thickly-set Doric columns, painted cream, measuring two feet in diameter, heavily fluted and emphatically

tapered, which upheld the story above. Adjoining the porch to its east was the horse path. This 20-feet wide passage bisected the ground floor of the Clubhouse and it was along this route that the horses and their riders walked from the Paddock to the track before each race *(Figure 64)*. The horse path and entry porch gave the building's ground floor an open, airy quality with an expansive outlook towards the greenery of the Paddock and the action of the track.

Further changes took place in the following decade. The 1930s was a decade of revitalization for thoroughbred racing at large. The populist anti-gambling sentiment of the late nineteenth and early twentieth centuries faded as the country was rocked by the Great Depression. In the wake of the crisis legalized gambling was suddenly looked upon as a quick-fire way to bolster the struggling economy and, eager to receive its lucrative revenues, one state after another legalized pari-mutuel wagering on horses in the 1930s. New York State followed this trend in 1939. Large, glamorous and ultra-modern racing facilities opened and thrived, exemplified by Santa Anita (opened 1934) and Hollywood Park (opened 1938) in California. No less attracted by the lure of easy money that wagering offered in penurious times, large crowds

Figure 65. Field Stand, built in 1936 and removed in 1963.

Figure 66. Betting Ring Grandstand extension, built 1937.

teemed at tracks old and new across the country. Growing numbers flocked to watch Saratoga's racing too, and once again the Saratoga Association found itself pushed to expand.

In 1936 the old Field Stand was razed and in its place rose a bigger, steel stand *(Figure 65)*. The replacement increased seating capacity by 500, to 1,200, and measured 116 by 30 feet. Furthermore, it introduced a new vocabulary of design to the course.

Bringing modern construction methods to Saratoga, the stand was a steel and concrete structure built to an economical design. The spartan building provided a single story of tiered seating accessed from the track apron by two sets of stairs. Unlike the Grandstand and Clubhouse, it had a flat roof supported by a row of six Y-shaped columns on the track side. Utilitarian in design, the rectangular stand was yet praised for its modernity. According to one contemporary, it was

the most uptodate feature of the racetrack and one that is appreciated by those unable to "pay the freight" at the regular grandstand and clubhouse. This Field Stand is a distinct attraction to racing at Saratoga for this class of patron. View of the track is adequate; refreshment and betting facilities are the best and field customers no longer need feel they have been "herded" into any old spot on the course.[90]

The field stand was dismantled in 1963; it leaves no impression on the physical environment on the Race Course today. Far more significant and lasting was the extension of the Grandstand's rear elevation, beginning in 1937. Although an addition had been tacked on to the 1892 Betting Ring in 1934, by 1936 the building was insufficient for Saratoga's many bookmakers and bustling crowds and architect Marcus T. Reynolds was hired to draw plans for a large Betting Ring extending from the back of the Grandstand. Reynolds was a leading Albany architect at a time when the city was experiencing its halcyon days. Although largely unsung since his death, Reynolds gave Albany some of its greatest landmarks including the imposing Flemish-gothic Delaware and Hudson Building, plus a Dutch Renaissance fire station, Italian palazzos and several classical banks. After his death in 1937, his firm was continued by his nephew, Kenneth Reynolds. The involvement of the practice at Saratoga would span almost a decade and would dramatically and permanently change the architectural character of the Frontside.

Ready to receive the crowds of the 1937 season, the Reynolds' extension consisted of a long, open structure bookended by two double-story rectangles perpendicular to the Grandstand. It was terminated at the east by a curved, one-story

Figure 67. Betting Ring terrace. Once open with views across the Back Yard, today the terrace is covered by red-and-white striped awnings.

entryway *(Figure 66)*. Running 360 feet in length and 85 feet deep, it vastly amplified the Grandstand.[91] The two "bookends" were shingle-clad structures, with a hipped metal roof with an ornamental scalloped edge. Metal roofing with scalloped edging was used again and again by the Reynolds firm at Saratoga. Wrapping around and extending between these two structures was a shed-row metal roof at

first floor level, which sloped down from a second-floor terrace. The terrace was a "summer garden", partially covered by a copper canopy, offering dining and refreshment facilities overlooking the Back Yard *(Figure 67)*. It was accessed directly from the Grandstand or via a double dog-leg staircase from the Back Yard *(Figure 68)*. The extension pioneered a new design aesthetic at the Spa. In sharp contrast with the dark wood and slate-roofed Victorian Grandstand and 1928 Clubhouse, the Reynolds addition made extensive use of metal roofs and ornamental white cast iron. This distinctive design aesthetic is now integral to the character of the Back Yard. The shed-row roof was upheld by decorative cast iron piers, imaginatively shaped into panels depicting racing scenes and horse-head brackets *(Figure 69)*. Matching cast-iron grilles railed the terrace, and was continued elegantly down the ornamental staircase to the Paddock. Whimsical, charming and unique to Saratoga, the ornamental iron work was a festive, jubilant addition to the racetrack. The clusters of flowers and shrubbery that poured over the terrace railings, the brightly-colored umbrellas that shaded the terrace tables, and Star Spangled Banner flying

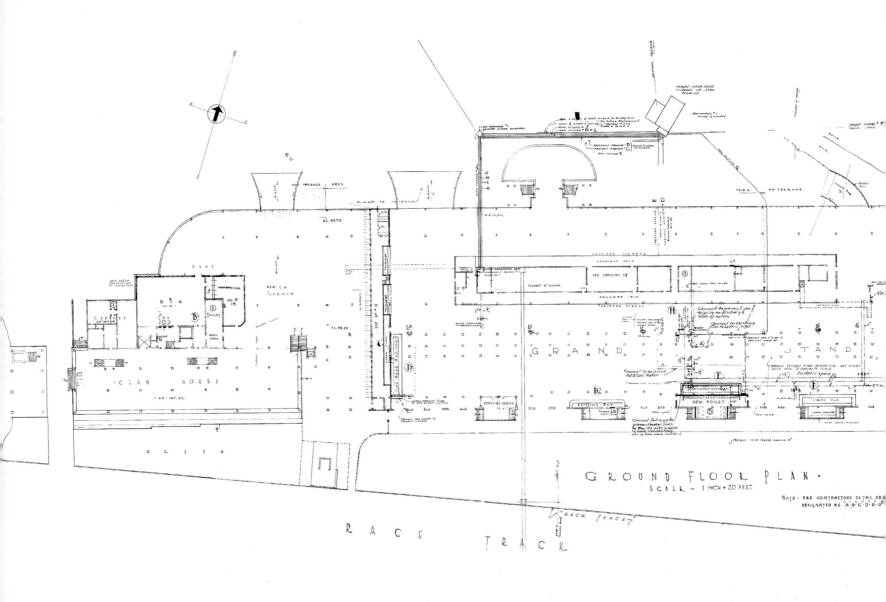

GROUND FLOOR PLAN.
SCALE - 1 INCH = 20 FEET

NOTE: SEE CONTRACTORS DETAIL DRAWINGS
DESIGNATED AS 'A' 'B' 'C' 'D' 'D' 'E'

CLUB HOUSE

OFFICES

TOILET

WASH ROOM

NEW C.H. TERRACE

GRAND STAND

STEVENS OFFICE

EXISTING BAR

NEW TOILET

RACE TRACK

TRACK FENCE

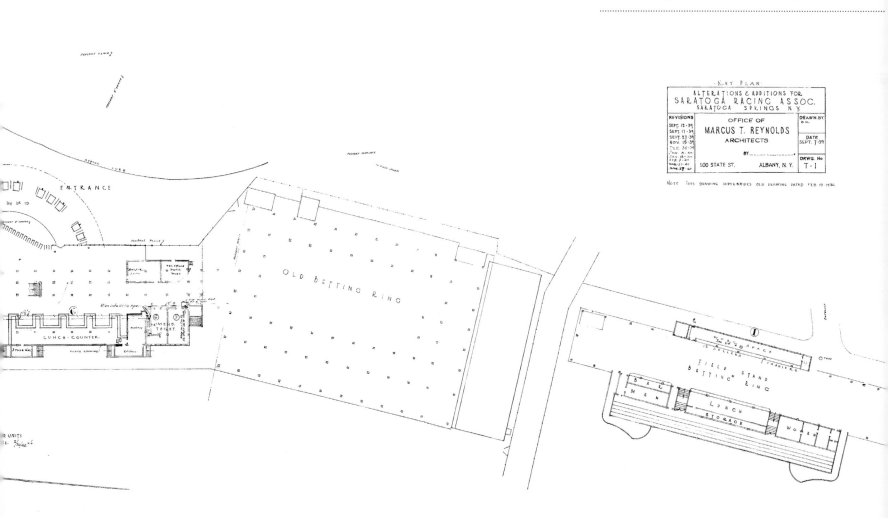

Figure 70. "Alterations and Additions for Saratoga Racing Association", Office of Marcus T. Reynolds, 1939.

atop the entrance all complemented this mood. The Reynolds involvement furthermore marked the transition from the tradition of deep, dark Victorian coloring towards bright white, painted surfaces. Not only was the extension painted white, but the rear and side elevations of the Grandstand and Clubhouse were too, resulting in the coloration familiar today.

Kenneth Reynolds, assuming the mantle of his late uncle, designed a further extension only two years later, which extruded the earlier Grandstand addition eastwards along the length of the Grandstand and westwards to link to the Clubhouse *(Figure 70)*. The proposals came to fruition several years later in the mid-1940s, when travel restrictions imposed by World War II forced the track to close between 1943 and 1945. Upon reopening in 1946, the extension was complete. The westward extension continued the second floor terrace to the rear of the Clubhouse, and ended in a curving termination at the rear kitchen annex. The impression of the Grandstand and Clubhouse, from the Back Yard at least, as a single continuous block was heightened. The vocabulary of ornamental cast iron work was introduced here also *(Figure 71)*. At ground floor level, cast iron posts bearing panels of equine

and Saratogian motifs with horse-head capitals upheld the sloping roof of the Betting Ring. Above, similarly ornamental iron rails interspersed with plantings enclosed the terrace. The Landing Stage, the Clubhouse's porch, was also embellished with the new design motifs. A curving extension was appended to meet the curving sweep of the entrance driveway, featuring the same decorative cast iron piers and also carved, horse-head, wooden brackets bearing a prominent cornice *(Figures 72, 73, 74, 75)*.

To contemporaries, the construction campaigns strengthened even further Saratoga's prestige within the thoroughbred world. Newspapers were full of the same histrionic enthusiasm with which they greeted the building campaigns under Walbaum and Whitney. It was "a wise move, racing experts, bookmakers, newspapermen and race fans in general agree," commended *This Week in Saratoga Life*.

Every detailed piece of reconstruction has been worked out to accomplish two purposes – elimination of crowded conditions and convenience to patrons and employees. And, at the same time, construction has been so modeled that rather than detracting from the natural beauty of the long-famous track it adds to the advantages by modern building in style of simple good taste.[92]

Saratoga's sleek new spaces provided the infrastructure for the arrival of the pari-mutuel to New York. After an overwhelmingly positive vote in 1939 to legalize pari-mutuel wagering in the state, pari-mutuel machines and infield tote

Figure 71. Elevation drawing of Betting Ring Clubhouse extension, Office of Marcus T. Reynolds, 1940.

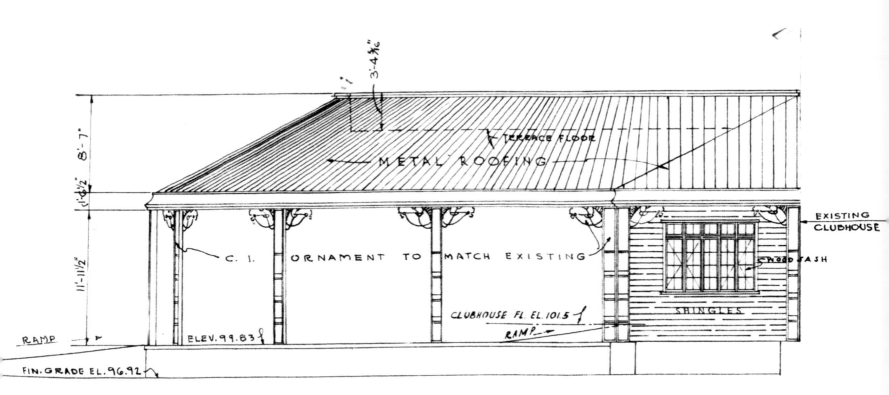

Figure 72. The "Landing Stage", the Clubhouse's exclusive entrance porch.

boards premiered at the Springs in summer 1940. Early pari-mutuel machines had in fact made an appearance at Saratoga during Morrissey's tenure, but had never replaced the bookmakers. This time, the change was permanent. Over $200,000 was spent readying the track. Nearly 300 betting and cashing windows were installed in the Grandstand complex, while more than 800 miles of cabling and 5,000 light bulbs were installed.[93]

With the old Betting Ring abandoned, its 1934 addition (120 by 35 feet) was transported to the rear of the new Field Stand and rotated 90 degrees. This was then extended to give the Field Stand a spacious betting space of its own. The original Betting Ring was turned over into a storage facility. At roughly the same time, a finish line camera was placed on the Clubhouse roof while freestanding camera towers rose around the track. A press box too was erected on the Grandstand roof "for as many newspaper men as the meeting will attract". Its facilities and view over the circuit may well have been "a distinct improvement on the old press box and result in better and more accurate accounts of local racing", but its aesthetic impact upon the Grandstand was decidedly less positive. The long box jutting from the stand's gray slate roof disrupted

Figure 73. Western façade of Clubhouse. The fountain was relocated here in 1928 from the main entrance.

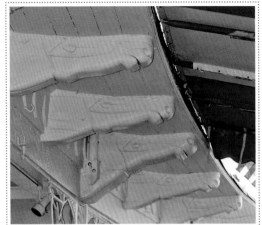

Figure 74. and Figure 75. The Office of Marcus T. Reynolds introduced a distinctive design vocabulary to the track, including carved wooden and cast iron horse-head brackets.

its sleek, sloping profile and the rupture was made even more pronounced by the bright white coloring of its shingle-clad walls.[94]

The track that reopened in 1946 after its war-years hiatus was in many ways a very different one to that in existence 20 years before. The 1920s, 30s and 40s were decades of significant building campaigns that had pronounced impacts upon the outer garb of the Frontside. Not least was the huge increase in building volume. The rebuilding of the Clubhouse and the two contiguous Betting Ring extensions created a much larger architectural footprint with advanced amenities to cater for Saratoga's growing legion of attendees. What is

more, its architectural complexion underwent a swingeing change. The robust and dark timber-framed structures of the Victorian age, exuding picturesque charm, were succeeded by a lighter, effervescent mood characterized by open terraces, cast-iron motifs and lashings of white paint. The repertoire of materials changed from slate and wood to structural steel and decorative metal, and the focus of the complex gradually began to veer from trackside to rear side. Despite the considerable change in footprint and architectural vocabulary, no long-term guiding plan steered this growth and no all-inclusive master study was undertaken of the complete property. Perhaps the undertaking

of some such study would have eliminated the inefficiency of constructing consecutive betting facility extensions in 1934, 1937 and 1943. To many, moreover, the growth spurt of these decades was not equal to the architectural and landscape highs of the Walbaum and Whitney eras and even compromised the elegance that these earlier generations had achieved in a quest for bigger, better and newer. Undoubtedly the loss of Warren's stylish 1892 Clubhouse was at the architectural cost of the Race Course, but Saratoga's gilded age heritage still survived at its heart. In spite of the encroachment of modern life upon the track's fabric, its romantic charm endured.

Figure 77. Today's Frontside

CHAPTER SEVEN
THE NEW YORK RACING ASSOCIATION

In August 1953 a group of sportsmen and members of the New York Racing Commission gathered for a dinner at Saratoga Race Course. The evening was to prove a far-reaching one. New York's racing had reached a nadir, the Commission's chairman Ashley Trimble Cole announced to the assembled company, and if the industry did not act quickly to reverse matters then the state would take control of the problem itself.

Since the Civil War, New York had been the leader in American racing. The charm, glamour and high-quality racing of the metropolitan Jerome, Morris and Belmont Parks and upstate Saratoga drew wealthy patrons and the best stables to the state. Yet by the mid-twentieth century, a handful of other states were challenging its crown. New Jersey's recently opened Monmouth Park was hugely

popular, whilst its Garden State Park track created the richest stakes race in the world, the Garden State Futurity. Rich purses were also on offer in Chicago. In 1953, the champion three-year-old Native Dancer earned $97,725 and $66,500 for winning the Arlington Classic and American Derby respectively at Chicago's Arlington Park; he received only $18,850 for victory at Saratoga's Travers Stakes. Native Dancer's appearance at the Travers drew a record attendance. Yet, even considering the celebrity of the equine star, a record crowd for Saratoga at this time was a mere 28,260 – an exceptionally modest figure given that today's Saratoga meeting averages nearly 22,000 attendees per day.[95] Both in prestige and financial health, the New York industry was flagging. Turfites feared for the very survival of Saratoga; it was earning the state less tax revenue than would a comparable downstate venue.[96]

Cole's pronouncement spurred New York's racing leadership into action. A committee was formed of three prominent entrepreneurs and Jockey Club members, John W. Hanes, Christopher T. Cheney and Harry F. Guggenheim, who promptly set about creating a new vision for racing within the state. They concluded that a non-profit corporation should be formed in order to purchase New York's four principal tracks – Saratoga, Belmont Park, Aqueduct and Jamaica. In so doing, they justified, the efficient operation of the tracks would be assured; the thoroughbred industry would be kept free of political influence whilst giving the state its fair share of revenue; and New York racing could be made competitive once more with the modernization of its facilities. In October 1955 their vision was inaugurated

as the Greater New York Association, quickly renaming itself the New York Racing Association (NYRA). It was granted a 25-year franchise to run the tracks on a not-for-profit basis.[97] In return, it received one per cent of the pari-mutuel revenue from the state's tax coffers to reinvest as track improvements. It was a new era for racing across the state.[98]

NYRA had big plans. Aqueduct was rebuilt as a state-of-the-art modern racing facility, completed in 1959; Jamaica was scheduled for closure as soon as the new Aqueduct was complete; Belmont Park was rebuilt from 1962-8, opening in time for the 100th running of the Belmont Stakes. Attendances at New York courses surged, and the money rolled in. Amidst this spurt of activity, though, Saratoga was left comparatively unheeded. By 1959, nearly $34 million had been spent on Aqueduct and over $7 million on Belmont Park, compared to $1 million on Saratoga. This may well have resulted from Saratoga's sequestered Hudson Valley location. Had the Adirondack Northway been complete by the 1950s, perhaps Saratoga's buildings too would have been razed in favor of a vast, contemporary, Aqueduct-like complex. Posterity can only be thankful for this accident of history.

NYRA did not forget its upstate track completely though. Following the transfer of the Race Course property to the new organization in 1955, work was immediately begun to improve its physical fabric. Several new stables and bunkhouses for track workers sprung up on both sides of Union Avenue, and private ownership of barns was promptly abandoned as NYRA bought up the stables surrounding the track. Subsequently, however, the construction of either bunkhouses or stables has been infrequent.[99] The building work marked the third phase in the evolution of Saratoga's backstretch. Compared to the backstretch's previous two periods of change in the nineteenth and earlier twentieth centuries, this third and final phase of its physical history was much less exertive. Overwhelmingly, the focus of NYRA's long-term improvement strategy was the public areas – the Frontside and Back Yard. In 1958 the Los Angeles firm Arthur Froehlich and Associates was engaged to make a study in view of expansion of the Grandstand and Clubhouse. Froehlich (1909-1985) was the premier designer of racetracks of the day. After completing his education at the University of California, Berkeley, he worked in the office

Figure 78. The Victorian Grandstand and its 1960s extension.

By the mid-1960s, Saratoga Springs and its racetrack began to be revived, and the track's venerable old Grandstand was no longer considered sufficient. It was at this time that Froehlich's study came to fruition. Led by architect Robert Krause, the new Grandstand was completed in 1965. The steel extension almost doubled the size of the wooden Grandstand. Directly abutting the east end of the Victorian Grandstand, the new building extended 500 feet to the east, necessitating the demolition of the Field Stand and Betting Ring, the latter having been stripped of its original function many years earlier. In an identical arrangement to the original structure, stadium-style seating was arranged in a tiered open story while betting booths were housed in the undercroft below. Direct passage was provided between the old stand and the modern portion, but nevertheless, the juncture was visually distinct *(Figure 78)*. The Froehlich firm was famed for its ultra-modern grandstands, sporting the most advanced amenities and construction techniques. It was less renowned for sensitive extensions to historic buildings, and this inexperience was pronounced at Saratoga. Whilst the Froehlich stand reproduced the elongated shape and height of the elevation of the Walbaum/Whitney era Grandstand, little attempt was made to achieve more than a superficial continuity between the new and the old. The steel frame of the addition was a marked contrast to the wooden trusses of the

of one of Los Angeles's leading architects, John Parkinson. As early as 1938, he had established his own practice which, in 1949, received the first of its many racetrack commissions, Hollywood Park in California. In little time, the firm had built an enviable reputation for the design of critically-acclaimed, cutting-edge horseracing facilities. By the

time of the Saratoga commission, the firm's racetrack portfolio included Roosevelt Raceway in New York and the Hipódromo La Rinconada in Venezuela, as well as the brand new Aqueduct. Nevertheless, for several years the plans for Saratoga lay untouched. NYRA's priorities lay with its downstate tracks, and it was to these that funding was directed.

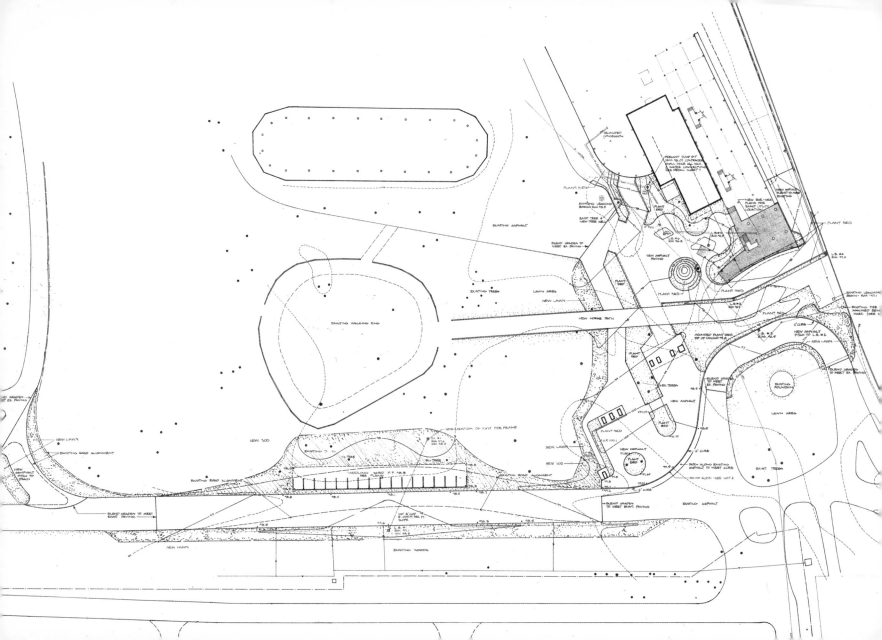

original building. The white painted elevation of the extension likewise differed from the reddish-brown stain of the old stand. Moreover, the beauty of the sweeping outlines of the Victorian Grandstand was not replicated. While two turrets capped with golden finials were incorporated into the roof of the new extension, the relationship between the 1965 stand and the 1902 structure was merely perfunctory. The latter had a gently curvilinear profile, but the 1960s roof was rigidly angular. Plus it was pitched at a milder angle, resulting in an awkward intersection between the two roofs. The structure was ultimately flawed by its insensitivity. The Grandstand may now have been fit to shelter modern crowds, but this was arguably at the expense of its quality of design.

The quality of the landscape surrounding the building was also, debatably, undermined by changes beginning in the 1960s. The previously open landscape, populated only by trees, was progressively colonized by a variety of small structures, sculpture, canopied television monitors, and picnic benches. A conspicuous arrival was an eccentric bandstand (later moved to the infield), fashioned solely from "found" materials such as copper balls from toilet tanks and chipboard bases of

Figure 80. "Going to the Post"

funeral wreaths. It was joined by the Big Red Spring, a large, neo-classical pavilion which was relocated to the western corner of the Back Yard in 1975. The gazebo had, in fact, begun life in 1859 sheltering a spring sited on Excelsior Avenue erected by the owners of the Excelsior Spring Water Company. In its new incarnation at the Race Course, it covered the track's own salubrious waters and was dedicated to popular favorite Man O'War.[100] The chestnut

colt, informally christened Big Red because of his coloring and stature, was sold as a yearling at Saratoga in 1918 and went on to make six out of his total 21 starts there, including his one and only defeat against the aptly-named Upset in the Sanford Memorial Stakes. The pavilion's presence and appellation illustrated the assertive sensibility of the track in embracing the history of the resort and its racing pedigree as a brand in itself.

The painted red-and-white coloration of the pavilion was idiosyncratic of the red-and-white character that the Frontside and Back Yard had increasingly assumed in the second half of the century. With the arrival of a series of red-and-white striped canopies across the Back Yard in the mid-1970s, this chromatic theme dominated the track's public areas and established an enduring brand image. The striped canopies, held aloft upon aluminum pipe frames, created covered walkways between the Grandstand and Clubhouse to the entrance gates and to the agglomeration of Back Yard structures. They were the result of a 1977 improvement plan by local architectural practice, The Saratoga Associates. The plan was to beget sizeable changes to the track's landscape environment. In particular, it yielded material alterations to the public's interaction with the Clubhouse. Since the construction of the Clubhouse in 1928, horses on their way from the Paddock to the track had traversed through its open ground floor between its colonnade of portly fluted columns at the western end. The 1977 changes saw this path re-routed outside the Clubhouse past its west façade, concurrently divesting the Clubhouse's porch of its original function as a circular drop-off driveway *(Figure 79)*. The vacated horse path and entry porch were converted into an extension of the dining facilities and the Travers Bar, akin to what exists today.

The Saratoga Associates' plans impacted not

Figure 81. Today's red-and-white striped canopied saddling shed was designed by architects The Saratoga Associates in 1977.

only upon the horse path, but upon the network of pathways across the Paddock as well. The 1977 campaign re-aligned Leavitt's 1902 peripheral road, straightening it alongside the property's western edge. Particularly in terms of this trajectory and the horse path, The Saratoga Associates superseded Leavitt's concept of meandering pathways with straight, direct circulation routes. The shifting of the perimeter road was a byproduct of a controversial modification

– the relocation of the saddling ceremony *(Figure 79)*. The 1902 Saddling Shed had been converted for pari-mutuel functions in 1963 but the saddling and walking continued in the open around the surrounding trees.[101] In 1977 the Saratoga Associates designed a new saddling tent alongside the western perimeter road. The steel-framed structure, sheltered by the endemic red-and-white striped canvas, pushed the pre-race ritual further westward and thus further

Figure 82. Racegoers watching the 21st-century pre-race Paddock parade behind fencing.

from the Back Yard's heart. For so many years, the saddling of champions under the lofty tree canopy where turf amateurs could rub elbows with jockeys and horses had held a staunch place in Saratoga tradition *(Figure 80)*. It was now an age of litigation, however, and concerns mounted that it was no longer safe to permit unrestricted public access to the horses for fear of injury. By 1986 a definite end was put to the tradition when, principally to protect onlookers

from loose horses, the walking ring and saddling tent were completely enclosed by fencing *(Figures 81, 82)*. Its abolition sent shock waves through Saratoga's veteran community.

The positive impacts of the 1977 and 1986 changes are hard to discern, but that the Back Yard and Clubhouse were being further and further distilled from the original essence of the place was clear. A clutter of temporary red-and-white striped canopies

interspersed with proliferating, straight pathways was replacing the simple, rustic elegance of the Race Course. Modernity had undoubtedly arrived at Saratoga and, to many eyes, was eroding its charm.

Meanwhile, NYRA was racked by financial difficulties. The association's inability to produce growth in revenues equal to the rate of growth of its expenses plagued its operations and the 1970s saw the beginning of an era of struggle which demanded continual legislative adjustment to keep NYRA buoyant in the face of the fluctuating handle and daily track attendances, and the inception of off-track betting (OTB). The arrival of OTB was a critical juncture in the fortune of all NYRA's tracks. Hitherto, legal wagering in New York had been confined to the placing of bets on the limited number of races that were run at the racetracks. In 1970, faced with a $630 million budget shortfall, Governor Nelson Rockefeller passed legislation which expanded the horse racing exemption to allow off-track betting in which pari-mutuel wagering could be conducted outside the confines of racetracks. The NYC OTB was created as a public benefit corporation, with a rationale that it would curb illegal bookmakers thus weakening organized crime and, moreover, that it promised the state a stream of revenue. Turf leaders howled in protest at this crippling drain to the tracks. By the end of its first operating year, OTB boasted a daily handle of $1.2 million and the corporation expanded quickly

The Froehlich firm was famed for its ultra-modern grandstands, sporting the most advanced amenities and construction techniques. It was less renowned for sensitive extensions to historic buildings, and this inexperience was pronounced at Saratoga.

in size, revenue and popularity. Conversely daily attendance at racecourses plummeted. The impact was long lasting, and the continual erosion of the fan base at the state's tracks proved a permanent source of oppression to NYRA's finances.

At this time, Saratoga was probably the lone bright spot in NYRA's finances. Between 1976 and 1983 Aqueduct's average daily on-track attendance had dropped from 20,722 to 13,340; in the same timeframe Belmont's daily average for its summer meeting had gone from 24,387 to 19,530; but Saratoga's figures had risen from 18,894 to 26,644. As the summer spectacle of the Saratoga meeting grew in popularity, accommodating the growing crowds at the track became a pressing concern spurring a series of architectural and landscape projects throughout the 1980s. This was, however, in the absence of a substantial revenue stream. A common theme of the physical evolution of the track in this and the ensuing decades was that each project was an individual undertaking unconstrained by any controlling master plan or

vision, such as had guided its development under William C. Whitney at the beginning of the century. Activity had been increasingly converging on the Back Yard since the 1960s, and to reflect this shift NYRA's new projects focused upon reorganizing the rear façade of the Grandstand complex. The works had a radical impact upon the complexion of the place. In 1980, the second floor terrace was enclosed by the ubiquitous red-and-white striped canopy upon a fixed steel frame creating an overflow area intended to hold 5,000 extra patrons. With the canopy in place, the open, outdoor space that the Reynolds firm had conceived in the 1930s and 40s was compromised, whilst views towards the iconic Grandstand roofline were checked. Equally, the canopy's low height impeded panoramic views from the terrace across the Back Yard.[102]

From 1985 to 1991, a great semicircular pavilion was erected extending from the rear of the Grandstand. Christened the Carousel Pavilion, it was a two-story building, open to the sides, providing food concessions, television monitors, and seating

designed by Philadelphia architects, Ewing Cole Cherry Parsky *(Figure 83)*. It mimicked the white horse-head bracket details and sloping standing seam metal roof of the Reynolds' era, yet it made for a lackluster addition to the track. Unlike the Reynolds' extensions, the cast iron horse heads had no supportive function and were applied decoratively to the outer face of the steel columns which upheld the structure. The Carousel Pavilion typified the tenor of NYRA's additions to the facility in that its design lacked sensitivity towards the subtlety of design of the track's architectural heritage and the quality of its construction materials. The result has been pastiche. Neither has the pavilion performed well commercially. It was intended as a vibrant food court destination but the space proved too deep and dark and racegoers have consistently preferred the open, rustic spaces of the Back Yard.

As embodied by the Carousel Pavilion, the changes to the track's physical fabric in the late twentieth century reflected an increasing desire

Figure 83. Carousel Pavilion, built 1985-91.

to provide modern amenities to entice the crowds. In 1985 plans were set forth to create a four-acre recreation area on the site of a grassed parking area near the Grandstand. The space featured a pari-mutuel pavilion with 40 betting windows, concession stands, television monitors, 100 picnic tables with umbrellas, and two admission areas, all sharing the red-and-white striped theme *(Figure 84)*. The intention was to create a part-picnic, part-festival showground in the leafy setting behind the Grandstand, where red and white umbrellas shaded picnicking families watching the racing from canopy-covered television sets.[103] The development marked the final realization of the Back Yard as a destination in its own right. A discernable shift in attitude was in evidence that the public should be catered for with a proliferation of souvenir booths, food and drink concessions and sanitary facilities. Notwithstanding the popularity of Saratoga's season, New York's pari-mutuel handle had declined more than 40 per cent between 1970 and 1991 (after inflation). With racing's traditional fan base ageing, the future seemed to lay in securing the "entertainment dollar". A report in the *Saratogian* at the height of the 1985 summer season abounded with the laudatory responses of the track patrons towards the new additions, particularly the television

monitors and picnic amenities. "It's like they made it for us," enthused one interviewee.[104] The picnic area is much loved and successful. However, by pushing Saratoga towards a venue of mass-entertainment, the elegant simplicity of the earlier eras of the course had waned. Eager to cater for the flourishing crowds and to health and safety precautions, the proliferation of stalls, betting booths and television screens that sprung up in the Back Yard lent to its historic acreage a cluttered and messy appearance. "The new area had more of everything," wrote Edward Hotaling, "except charm."[105]

Twenty-first-century plans reveal the fading of the open, transparent quality for which the Back Yard had been known until comparatively recently. By the turn of the millennium, a network of paths led between the Kasbah-like assortment of canopied buildings and concession stands. Fences lined the horse path from Union Avenue to the saddling Paddock and the Frontside. Saratoga's legendary elms, maples and pines still towered over the property, particularly in the land between the Union Street entrances, but pervasive hardscaping around the Grandstand-Clubhouse complex had contracted the tree canopy. The rural idyll of Saratoga's Back Yard was quickly succumbing to blacktop.

Neither has the historic backstretch been immune from the spread of paving. The dirt tracks that spanned Horse Haven were indicative of the age in which it developed, but by the late twentieth century horsemen and security officials used cars to navigate the site. To facilitate this, in 1984 the roadway into Horse Haven was blacktopped. The route traversed the original 1847 trotting oval at two points, so in paving the roadway the track's traditional role as a training circuit for young horses was rendered defunct. The step was immediately questioned by horsemen as well as local preservationists. It resulted in more horses on the Oklahoma track, necessitating horses to circumnavigate it in two directions.[106] The introduction of asphalt paving within the backstretch has slowly continued. Compounded with the proliferating use of cars, this resurfacing is gradually having a serious impact upon the health of the Race Course's tree population. With automobile parking completely ungoverned, tree roots are smarting from soil compaction. This insensitivity to the landscape prompted especial vitriol within the 2010 Cultural Resources Inventory commissioned by the Saratoga Springs Preservation Foundation. "Re-surfacing activities continuously threaten the lives of many of Horse Haven's trees," authors Martha Lyons and Kim Alvarez wrote, "risking

the loss of the area's most outstanding character-defining landscape features."[107]

Continuing the steady stream of episodic improvement works upon the Race Course property, in 2000 attention was turned to the arrival experience. Using designs by The Saratoga Associates, three new public entrances were erected, two on Union Avenue and one on Wright Street, west of the Clubhouse. Substantial in size, the sloping, slate-covered hipped roofs of the three gateway structures carried echoes of the spirit of the Race Course's golden eras. They were designed as airy pavilions, upheld by white-painted timber frames upon brick bases and were surrounded by spacious, geometrically-planned, hardscaped plazas. At the Wright Street gate this included the nineteenth-century fountain that had previously been sited at the Clubhouse entrance (Figure 85).

The three, visually imposing entrance pavilions typified the nature of Saratoga's evolution in the second half of the twentieth century. Their realization was approached in isolation; no overarching vision existed for the land. Indeed, no comprehensive full-site master plan had been commissioned since that produced in 1902 under the

aegis of the visionary William C. Whitney. Whitney and his landscape engineer, Charles Leavitt, endowed the track with a lasting architectural and landscape framework, which continues to shape the skeleton of the Race Course we know today. However, since the late 1920s, growth within the environs of the Frontside has not been guided by any such master plan; its absence has proved telling. Particularly since the 1970s, the incremental mushrooming of television monitors, concession stands, and labyrinthine pathways has diluted much of the overall coherency of the site. Its pastoral charm, for which Saratoga has so long been famed, is at risk from carnivalesque bacchanalia and blacktop.

The challenge of operating Saratoga has been by no means easy for NYRA. When funding was plentiful in the 1950s and 1960s, the Race Course was unfashionable and so not a priority for investment. In recent decades, whilst the track's prestige has rallied, NYRA has faced a series of financial and political crises which blocked investment. By the mid 1990s the association's revenues had stagnated. It was facing increasing competition from other racetracks and other forms of gambling, plus it lost a substantial market share

Figure 84. Back Yard picnic area, created in 1985.

Light at the end of the tunnel appeared in 2001 when New York State legislature authorized the construction of a video lottery terminal (VLT) facility at Aqueduct Racetrack. NYRA was not alone in its deficits; the state too was struggling to balance its books and, akin to the legalization of pari-mutuel wagering in the 1930s and OTBs in the 1970s, VLT was held as a lucrative white knight both for the state and NYRA. The years passed though and no VLTs appeared at Aqueduct. NYRA had long had a difficult relationship with the state, and the latter repeatedly delayed granting approvals for construction to begin.

In 2003, NYRA was indicted on charges of tax evasion and money laundering. The outlook looked bleak. Yet, the episode in many ways marked a turning point for the association. It was placed under a deferred prosecution order, which wielded a strict set of constraints. NYRA embarked upon a period of self-reform, going above and beyond these constraints. It implemented new cash-handling procedures, launched a comprehensive anti-money-laundering education program, took a hard line against illegal performance-enhancing drugs, and extensively restructured its management, amongst other measures. Insolvency, though, was looming. By 2005, NYRA was operating at a net loss of $22 million. Grudgingly, state officials granted a $30 million loan which removed the immediate shadow of bankruptcy but did not give sufficient latitude

to OTB facilities. Expenses, however, continued to rise. The cost of maintaining Aqueduct, Belmont Park and Saratoga, not to mention funding purses, subsumed a vast portion of the organization's revenue. A lengthy roll call of taxes, fees and pension-deficit payments mandated by federal and state law subsumed most of the rest. Most stiflingly, the terms of the franchise which authorized NYRA to operate New York's three

major tracks compelled it to pay the state all of its adjusted annual net income bar $2 million. This $2 million had not only to support periods of negative cash flow but was also the sum total allotted to fund improvement works at the three tracks. Without spending power, NYRA was blocked from implementing large-scale capital works to any of its facilities. Small-scale projects and ad hoc measures were the only affordable options.[108]

Figure 85. Wright Street entrance gates, built in 2000.

to plan for any long-term improvement works at Saratoga, nor at any of its tracks. To compound matters, its 2007 franchise was up for renewal.[109]

NYRA had long been plagued with a chronic franchising problem. Upon its formation in 1955, the association was granted a 25-year franchise by the State Legislature to operate its tracks. This long-term agreement gave NYRA the freedom, both in terms of time and economics, to embark upon extensive capital improvement projects. The nature of any architectural and landscape works at Saratoga and its sister tracks in the last quarter of the twentieth century was, however, strongly governed by the inability to secure another such agreement. At the expiration of the original franchise, NYRA was granted a series of short-term extensions to 1987, to 1994, to 2000 and to 2007. This succession of interim continuations is directly correspondent to the piecemeal nature of the development works that took place at Saratoga Race Course in these years. As the 2007 franchise approached expiration, other serious contenders were waiting in the wings to usurp NYRA and it was by no means certain that the state would renew the association's franchise. After months of speculation, however, this is exactly what they did.

Without spending power, NYRA was blocked from implementing large-scale capital works to any of its facilities. Small-scale projects and ad hoc measures were the only affordable options.

On February 13, 2008, the New York State legislature granted NYRA an extension of 25 years. This was no small achievement. NYRA's fortunes were looking up. It received $105 million in direct state aid and millions more in loans were cancelled in return for relinquishing to the state any claims to ownership of the land upon which the three racetracks are sited. This involved a transfer of assets to the state of $1 billion. And finally, in 2010, after a taxing and prolonged political, legal and financial struggle, a

contract for a VLT facility at Aqueduct was signed. The VLTs are set to open in 2011, providing NYRA with a considerable capital injection.

The Springs has already been confirmed as a priority target for this capital and conditions are ripe for its venerable track to enter a renaissance. Together, the 25-year franchise offers much-needed stability – which had been unachievable during the previous short-term agreements – and the VLTs provide the funds to create a platform for the implementation of a new master plan at Saratoga Race Course, the first in over a century. Encompassing each aspect of the Race Course, from its stables, to its circuits to its public buildings and Back Yard, the master plan is set to address the property as a coherent whole and to shape the future of its physical evolution for decades to come. The track is entering a critical juncture in its evolution; posterity may well reveal it to be no less critical than the rebirth of the Saratoga Association under Whitney's leadership in 1901. As North America's most important racing meeting, what happens next at Saratoga Race Course will define the future of New York thoroughbred racing and create a guiding light for the sport nation-wide.

CONCLUSION:
SARATOGA'S LEGENDARY TRACK

For 45 weeks of the year, life in Saratoga Springs rumbles peacefully onwards amidst gracious Victorian mansions and tree-bowered roads. But in late July, the town catches turf fever. With the start of the racing season, its population triples. Everybody thinks horses, talks horses, breaths horses. It is the Kentucky Derby or Royal Ascot, not for one day or five days but for forty. The very name of Saratoga causes pulses to beat quicker. What would John "Old Smoke" Morrissey think upon hearing that the experimental thoroughbred meeting he engineered nearly 150 years ago now draws over 800,000 visitors annually? Saratoga Race Course has gripped the nation's imagination since the nineteenth century; no other track has sustained its standing in the hearts and minds of racing fans for such a length of time. But why?

In an age when sports traditions are more manufactured than made, Saratoga's spirit of romance and history stands as a beacon. Its status as America's oldest sporting venue is no empty rubric – it is tangibly embodied in its buildings, landscape and ambience. At its heart sits the iconic silhouette of the Victorian Grandstand, with its sweeping, turreted roofline and robust yet picturesque timber frame; adjoining sits the 1928 Clubhouse and additions from succeeding decades, united by white wrought-iron equine-themed decoration that perfectly embodies the jubilant spirit of the place. Across the main track, the village of stables dates back as far as the 1840s. And the whole ensemble is set within inspiring groves of maples, pines and elms, making welcome shade from the summer sunshine. The Race Course is a multi-layered tapestry of trees and buildings, a visible product of decades worth of growth from the days of the earliest trotting track in the 1840s, to the heady (and ignominious) chapter of Gottfried Walbaum's ownership, to William C. Whitney's transformations, and finally to the present tenure of NYRA. Its physical environment tells the story of changing architectural fashions, the evolution of the sport itself, the ebbs and flows of Saratoga the township, and the vibrant personalities who have trod, owned and shaped these hallowed grounds. At Saratoga, history can be seen, touched and sensed.

At no other racetrack in the country, perhaps at no other track in the world, is history so palpable. Saratoga stands alone amongst its peers because throughout its lifetime it has resisted the urge to raze and rebuild bigger and better. Take Ascot, for example, possibly the most celebrated racing venue the world across. Its foundation stretches back to 1711 – more than a century and a half before Saratoga Race Course was even a glimmer in John Morrissey's eye – when Queen Anne ruled that the Berkshire heath was the perfect spot for racing. Ascot's first permanent building was erected in 1793, whilst it even sported the work of Georgian Britain's most distinguished architect, John Nash, who designed a Royal Stand in 1822. However, not a trace of either survives. We can read it in the history books but we cannot see it with our eyes. Twice in the past 50 years alone, Ascot has been subject to a wholesale redevelopment where all vestiges of its grandstand and paddock were demolished in the quest for modernized facilities. Churchill Downs provides another pertinent comparison. Some may argue that the Louisville track, as home to America's most celebrated race, ranks as the nation's most historic racetrack. If there is one image that captures the spirit of American racing more than any other, it is the twin spires of Churchill Downs' 1895 grandstand. Yet expand this